Captive in Formosa

A British P.O.W.'s struggle for survival, 1942–1945

by
Norman Cliff

By the same Author
Courtyard of the Happy Way
Hijacked on the Huangpu

© N. H. Cliff 1993
British Library Cataloguing-in-Publication Data. A catalogue record for this book is available from the British Library.
N. H. Cliff 1925 –
ISBN 1 898881 00 6

Published by
The Rochford Press Limited
Unit 7, Riverside Industrial Estate, South Street, Rochford, Essex. SS4 1BL. (0702) 548681
in association with **Robert Odcombe Associates**

This book
is dedicated to
Joyce

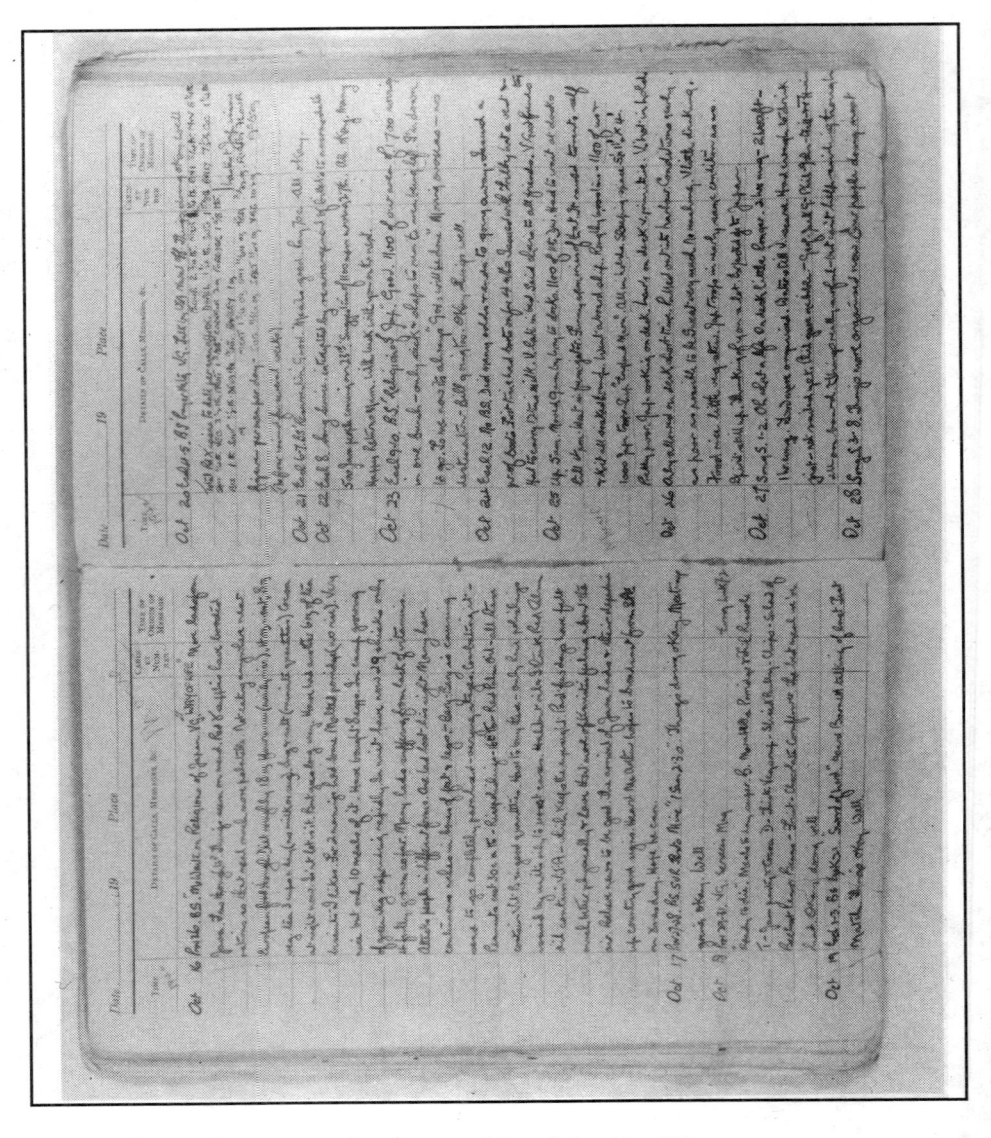

Two pages from Lionel Haylor's Diary (Oct. 16 - Oct 28)

INTRODUCTION

On my desk lies a tattered diary - a precious record which Lionel Haylor kept throughout his 3½ years as a prisoner-of-war. If this thin volume could tell its own story the events of this book could be recounted more eloquently and more vividly than I could possibly do, as a mere second-hand writer of this important story.

To keep a note book or diary was specifically forbidden under Japanese camp regulations, and anyone who ignored this ruling was clearly looking for trouble. The Japanese guards went regularly into the prisoners' huts and carried out a tenko and search. Sometimes there would be sufficient time to put the book quickly into a "hide-hole". While a prisoner was waiting to be searched he could hear shouts and screams from a neighbouring hut, and then a man would be dragged out to the parade ground and face severe punishments for keeping a forbidden article, which might be a roll of wire, a sharpened piece of metal, a note book or a diary. When the guards came to a man's hut his heart would stay in his mouth while they poked and prodded the clothing and blankets, and inspected his few belongings.

If a diary was found it was confiscated and taken to the Japanese office, and with the help of an interpreter would be studied page by page. The owner would later be sent for and asked such searching questions as "Where did you get the war news from?" or "Is there a hidden radio?" Where nicknames had been used for the guards the prisoner would be asked to decode the references, and the guards could get angry at the statements recorded.

Lionel Haylor bravely broke the camp regulations and faithfully kept his own personal record of his hopes and fears, his faith and his doubts, his fluctuating health and the sordid conditions under which he was incarcerated in four military camps - the latter three all in Taiwan - during World War II.

With each move he succeeded in keeping his diary, in spite of regular searches. One of his tactics was to divert the guard's attention from the contents of his rucksack by displaying photos of his fiancee and his family. These invariably aroused their interest and fostered goodwill.

If the diary could speak it would have told how it was nearly destroyed in company with its owner when American planes dropped bombs on Takao Camp six months before the end of the war. Shrapnel was embedded into the book, leaving some pages torn and dishevelled. It is largely from this tattered book that this fascinating story has been told.

We are indebted to Lionel Haylor for keeping such a faithful record and sharing it with us.

ACKNOWLEDGEMENTS
Diary of L. Haylor
Diary of Dr. Ben Wheeler
The Story of Changi – D. Nelson
The Road from Singapore – D. Norman
Banzai you Bastards – J. Edwards
Formosa (Taiwan) – W. G. Goddard
Taiwan in Modern Times – P. K. T. Sih

FOREWORD

This book is the story of a man's struggle for survival during one of the bleakest periods of modern history.

In the same war, but in a different place, Viktor Frankl also struggled for survival against all the odds. He wondered why some survived and others did not. It was not a matter of physical strength - some of the strongest were among the first to succumb to disease and despair. He came to the conclusion that having something to live for was all important: tasks to complete, loved ones to be re-united with, a faith, which however dimly held, could give some meaning to the experience.

You will find all those things echoed in this account of Lionel Haylor's captivity in Formosa. Significantly, Frankl also set himself to the task of reconstructiong on tiny scraps of paper a manuscript which had been confiscated when he was arrested - not unlike the diary which Lionel Haylor kept during the time of his imprisonment, and which now forms the basis of Norman Cliff's story.

This is a privileged glimpse of a man's courage and faith at a time of utmost testing. To re-live those days, and to share them with others, cannot be without questions and pain, but it is important that such stories are told. In a world where there is still more than enough of man's inhumanity to man it is good to be reminded that the human spirit is capable of reaching the heights as well as plumbing the depths.

We are grateful to Lionel Haylor for his willingness to share the story of these eventful years. I commend his story to you.

Alwyn Knight
(Minister, Wester Road United Reformed Church, Romford).

CONTENTS

Introduction v
Acknowledgements vi
Chapter 1.   Change at Changi 1
              (Changi Camp 17/2/42 – 24/10/42)
        2.   Blueprints for Survival 7
        3.   Marching Orders to go East 11
              (Voyage 25/10/42 – 13/11/42)
        4.   The Rigours of Taihoku Camp, Formosa 17
              (Taihoku Camp 14/11/42 – 11/11/43)
        5.   Taichu Camp and the Arrival of Mail from Home 35
              (Taichu Camp 12/11/43 – 28/6/44)
        6.   Takao Camp and the Progress of the War 39
              (Takao Camp 29/6/44 – 11/3/45)
        7.   Surviving the Last Lap 45
              (Taichoku Camp 12/3/45 – 6/9/45)
Epilogue 51
Appendices 55
        1.   Numerical Strength of Changi Camp, 17/2/42 – 31/10/43. 56
        2.   The Selarang Special Order. 57
        3.   The Japanese Order to kill all P.O.W.s in Formosa. ... 59
        4.   Obituary to John Burns Leech. 62
        5.   L. Haylor's Weight, 16/9/42 – 31/1/46. 63
List of Maps
        1.   The Voyage from Changi Camp, Singapore,
            to Taihoku Camp, Formosa 13
        2.   Japanese P.O.W. Camps in Formosa 21
List of Illustrations
        Pages from Lionel Haylor's Diary iv
        Lionel Haylor 26
        Life in Taiwan Camps 27
        Cover of Soldier's Service and Pay Book 30
        Inside Lionel Haylor's Soldier's Service and Pay Book 31
        Cover of W/T Operator's Log 32
        Page of Lionel Haylor's Allowance Book 33
        Wedding of Lionel and Joan Haylor 54

Chapter 1.
Change at Changi

(Changi Camp 17/2/42 – 24/10/42)

15th February, 1942, was a bleak day indeed. The strategic and populated island of Singapore was lying in ruins after fifteen days of intense fighting.

There was a pall of black smoke covering the island. The once prosperous city and its docks were strewn with rubble, and the bodies of civilians and soldiers lay in the streets. There were abandoned cars and lorries strewn across the roads. Frightened groups of civilians were clambering over the broken bricks and through the gaps between the damaged buildings to get to safety.

The Japanese, though outnumbered by the Allied forces, had advanced southwards from Malaya and cut off the island's water supply. The unwelcome fact was that SINGAPORE HAD SURRENDERED TO THE JAPANESE. It was part of that hundred days of unbroken success. Following the raid on Pearl Harbor the enemy had had a series of astounding successes.

Slowly the noise of gunfire and bombing began to subside. Signalman Lionel Haylor wrote tersely in his diary:

Sunday. 15 Feb. 1942. Ceasefire 8.30 p.m. Relieved to know no more fighting. Was pleased to hand over rifle.

He knew he was going into captivity and that Japan was winning on all fronts. But, with typical British optimism and self-confidence he thought it would be a matter of months rather than years before the Allies would win the war. The next day he recorded in his diary that he had seen his first Japanese. The soldier was *"looking scruffy"*, but he quickly added - *"so do we"*. In the next three and a half years he was to see plenty of these short bow-legged men in all kinds of circumstances. But his first impressions were favourable. Lionel wrote, *"We seem to be treated very well."*

At 2 p.m. on Tuesday he began a twelve-mile march from the north of the island to prison camp. It was a hot sticky day, and as the march proceeded the column got longer and longer as more units joined the crocodile procession. The roads were rough and they clambered over bricks and rubble scattered on their route from the recent fighting. Marching through the city, Lionel noticed that many Chinese shopkeepers were dutifully hanging Japanese flags outside their businesses. It was a tiring march, and his feet were swollen and blistered. The soldiers were allowed a few pauses, and when they came he carefully adjusted his socks and boots. On the road again marching into the great unknown, his thoughts went to Joan back in Romford, Essex. The day fixed for their wedding at the Congregational Church was not far away, but events were threatening to hinder this happy event from happening on the due date. Should he plan an escape ... but he had no local contacts and spoke none of the local languages.

They arrived in the dark at Changi Camp - so this is it. They were hot, tired, dirty and hungry, but the need for sleep eclipsed all other considerations. The signalman unpacked his kit and lay out his blankets on the concrete floor, and lay side by side with hundreds of fellow soldier prisoners, and slept till sunrise.

When he awoke he ate his ration of tinned beef and canned vegetables, which the army had brought to camp on the previous day's march. He then surveyed his new surroundings. They were in a large military barracks which had been badly damaged in the recent fighting. There were big gaping holes in the walls and roofs of the bungalows. No less than 30,000 troops had arrived that first Tuesday, and within a few weeks, as groups of stragglers from the Malayan jungle and survivors from torpedoed ships arrived in small and large batches, the numbers were to swell to no less than 52,000. There were many sick and wounded among them who were taken to a makeshift hospital. Four miles away hundreds of civilian prisoners - men, women and children - were crowded into a former prison.

Without a shirt on and hobbling on his swollen feet, Lionel went with hundreds of other prisoners out into the boiling sun to clear up the debris, and bring some kind of order to the chaos from the recent fighting. It was dangerous work - there were shells amongst the rubble which was to be disposed of. Later they received their first issue of rice which was to become their staple diet. It was to be some weeks before their stomachs would accept this new form of nourishment.

During the days which followed, life in this massive prison camp gradually took some form of order. Barbed wire was secured around the large perimeter, and Japanese armed guards were soon patrolling the camp walls twenty four hours a day. The area within the camp was divided into compartments with about 2,500 men in each unit; and there was to be no communication between one unit and another. Working parties of those classified as fit went out each day to build roads, whilst the partially fit were detailed to work in the camp kitchen or do sanitation work.

Initially the food position was fair. The small rations of rice which the prisoners were issued could be supplemented with the supplies which they had brought with them to Changi. But water which was fit for drinking was scarce from the very beginning. It came in watercarts, chlorinated and very strictly rationed. The water in the wells had been contaminated by corpses from the siege and from decaying vegetables. The medical officers watched this problem with the utmost caution. If careful instructions were not regularly given to the soldiers there could be a serious health crisis. But later the water supplies were to improve.

In the Far East fighting zone the Japanese Army was tightly stretched. They were fighting on many fronts, and with the capture of new countries their commitments were exceeding the men who were available. Men who had been trained to do battle were being wasted watching over enemy prisoners. Lionel wrote in his diary -

31 Mar. 1942. Japs established Free Indian Army. About 700 Sikhs have gone over to it.

Gradually the Japanese camp guards were phased out to be replaced by Sikhs and Bengalis. But for the prisoners, both military and civilian, this change brought worsened conditions. There was now face slapping and regular cases of brutality. British officers working in the camp administration office acted quickly, and requested the return of the Japanese guards, and it was to be some weeks before the change was reversed. This request sounds strange in view of later developments in all the Japanese camps, but it was a case of "Better the devil you know than the devil you don't know."

The supplies of tinned beef, canned vegetables and biscuits which the various regiments had brought into Changi, and which had supplemented their small meals was soon used up, and rice became the main diet, although the stomachs of most prisoners still resisted it. Only occasionally did bread come in, and when it did it was most welcome.

Lionel was limping with a septic leg through an injury received while working on the roads, and then experienced severe stomach pains through the new diet which was both inadequate and unhygienic. The following extracts from his diary show that conditions were already critical -

    3 Mar. 1942. *Food here is a big question. Many chaps are sick, seemingly change of food. If sickness increases disease may spread.*
    6 Mar. 1942. *What a pain in tummy.*
    22 Mar. 1942. *Tummy still not behaving.*
    15 Apr. 1942. *One chap in dock with beri beri.*
    17 May 1942. *Tummy off colour.*

In fact the records show that by as early as 13th March, after less than a month of imprisonment, there had already been as many as 800 cases of dysentery and 28 deaths. As the months went by vitamin deficiency diseases and illnesses caused by bad food, bad water and bad sanitation were to take their toll in Changi. Lionel was to later record -

    23 Sept. 1942. *Three chaps in hospital blind through our diet.*

Blindness from vitamin deficiency was to become increasingly commonplace. Also regularly during his time at Changi the prisoner put down in his diary "*Another chap died today*".

The food position, though never satisfactory, fluctuated from one day to the next, as the following extracts from Lionel's diary will show -

    6 Apr. 1942. *Meals poor.*
    7 Apr. 1942. *Better meals.*
    10 Apr. 1942. *Oh boy, what a feed. Had a bread roll covered in marmalade after dark. I likes. R. Pryke got some eats from Singapore.*
    7 May. 1942. *Slightly better ration issue.*
    22 May, 1942. *Roast meat for dinner - good.*
    23 May. 1942. *Pie for dinner - good.*

By June, 1942, two factors combined to improve the critical food problem. Prisoners were paid wages for their labour on the roads and buildings, and a canteen was opened where they could purchase items of food - eggs, blachan (shrimp paste), gula melaka (sugar from a local palm), pineapples and bananas. And so from this time on Lionel is frequently recording in his diary - "*Pay day 70c ... Bought 2 eggs ... Things O.K.*" But in spite of this improvement, the records show that many prisoners are suffering from beri beri and dysentery.

By September the camp was going through another crisis through lack of food, and the arrival of Red Cross parcels in mid-October gave the prisoners a brief respite.

    13 Oct. 1942. *Red Cross supply - 17 lbs per man. This food a real God-send in real sense. Cos we were on last legs re. rations.*
    16 Oct. 1942. *Red Cross supplies have boosted rations. In camp growing green vegetables. Have 29 chicks. Many lads suffering from lack of vitamins.*

Attacks people in different forms. One lad lost his sight. Many have continuous aches in bones of feet and legs. Beri beri is causing some to go completely paralysed.

Six months after the prisoners had been in Changi Camp an incident took place in which the Japanese used their military might to force them to conform to their demands.

At the end of August, 1942, some forms arrived in the camp from Japan. They read, "I, the undersigned, hereby solemnly swear on my honour that I will not, under any circumstances, attempt to escape." The order was that every inmate must sign such a form. But British Army Regulations required that military prisoners should escape from P.O.W. camps if they considered it possible. Thus orders from the Japanese conflicted with military regulations. Which should be obeyed?

In many other camps in the Far East prisoners had in fact signed such forms on the grounds that living conditions were already bad enough, and any refusals would immediately bring less rations, less camp privileges and closer surveillance; also that signing such a document under duress did not bring with it any moral commitment. Lionel's diary reads-

> 1 Sept. 1942. *Paper to sign from Japan. All refused to sign. Against Army regulations.*

This unanimous decision by the prisoners was conveyed by the camp administration to the Japanese. Their response was swift and firm. On the morning of 2nd September the 16,000 prisoners were given orders to move out of Changi by noon, to take only what they could carry, and if they were not in Selerang Barracks by 6 pm.. they would be shot dead.

Soon the march out of Changi had begun. Thousands of bedraggled prisoners were wending their way in an endless chain the few miles to Selerang. On arrival they were crammed as tight as tight could be - a batch of a thousand into a building 120 feet by 80 feet. Some even slept on the roofs. Barbed wire was erected around them, and patrols of Japanese and Indian guards marched around them with fixed bayonets.

They were truly at the mercy of their captors. They had only the food which they had brought with them. There was no water for washing or cleaning, and there were no toilets. Lionel was working *"digging slit latrines in middle of square ... digging at night as well."* When he did have a few moments he read the Bible at the point where he had been reading at that time, and found these words -

> O Lord, my God, in Thee do I put my trust. Save me from all them that persecute me, and deliver me. Lest he tear my soul like a lion, rending it in pieces, while there is none to deliver.   (Psalm 7, vv. 1,2)

He commented, *"encouraging verses"*. He realised that the threats and pressures of General Fukuei Shimpei could only harm him up to a point, and no further.

The senior prisoner, a colonel, after consultation with other officers, then told the Japanese that he would instruct all prisoners to sign their forms. Lionel wrote -

> 4. Sept. 1942. *Papers handed out and signed in evening ... though the paper means nothing to me.*

Under these enormous pressures the prisoners had capitulated. The Japanese then arranged for them to return to Changi.

> 5 Sept. 1942. *Orders to move 1 p.m. Things all packed up and toddle off to old camp. Very tired by evening time. Still it's been an experience. Back to normal, I hope.*
>
> 6 Sept. 1942. *Very relieved to be back in own billets. Rations came up. Very good ration.*

At this time the prisoners-of-war felt increasingly at the mercy of their captors. On the morning of the very day they marched to Selerang Fukuei had ordered that four prisoners who had been found outside the barbed wire be shot. Then upon their return to Changi he ordered that all prisoners who were in buildings adjacent to the sea be moved, and there was consequently a general reshuffle. The inmates were slowly learning the hard lesson that conformity to camp regulations and the guards' orders were essential to their survival, and that any variation from them brought upon their heads penalties which were both severe and drastic.

The actions of Fukuei in moving thousands of prisoners to Selarang and back to Changi within a few days were like those of the famous Grand Old Duke of York -

> *O the Grand Old Duke of York,*
> *He had ten thousand men,*
> *He marched them up to the top of the hill,*
> *And he marched them down again.*

But the Japanese General lived to regret what he had done. Three years later he was to be brought before a War Crimes Tribunal, and was shot by a firing squad for his cruel deeds in Singapore.

Chapter 2.
Blueprints for Survival

For many prisoners at Changi the perpetual hunger, debilitating illness, cramped accommodation and the general discomfort of daily life brought about a surprising change in their personalities. Embittered by recent experiences, full of self pity about their harsh circumstances and pessimistic about what the future held for them, they abandoned their principles and became involved in gambling, stealing food and in such activities as the drug traffic.

Lionel Haylor, perhaps unconsciously, formed some blueprints for survival in these sordid conditions. First and foremost there was the spiritual side of his life. His diary shows that he attended the camp service every Sunday as well as the weekly Bible Study. He would record the subject of the sermon at the service, and the subject discussed at the Bible Study. Two months after his imprisonment he made a significant entry in his diary -

> 18 Apr. 1942. *Bible study good. Very good talk with missionary Mr. Leech afterwards. Views clearing and sorting themselves.*

Lieutenant John Leech was a remarkable Christian man, and Lionel's meeting him was to have a profound influence on his life. At the age of 16 Leech had joined the British Army and gone to India. Four years later he had experienced a Pauline conversion, so that as soon as he could get his release he went to a missionary training college in Britain, and then joined the Regions Beyond Missionary Union, who sent him to his old stamping ground in north India. But at the outbreak of war he had been called back to military service.

Leech did not have the polished rhetoric and intellectual powers of the regular padre, but his strong evangelical faith was contagious, and he was able to explain the doctrines of the Bible in the simplest terms. Lionel had heart to heart talks with this missionary, and he could not help but catch some of the fervour and certainty of Leech's strong faith. The following selections from the diary will show some steps in the young prisoner's spiritual pilgrimage after his contact with John Leech -

> 20 May 1942. *Gave life in service to the Lord Jesus Christ.*
> 28 May 1942. *Padre little better*
> 30 May 1942. *Went to hospital to visit instead of padre.*
> 7 Jun 1942. *Genesis 1 - 4. Started reading Bible cover to cover.*
> 17 Aug 1942. *Song service in chapel. I had to take service.*

During the remainder of his time in Changi prison Lionel had many deep talks with John Leech. For Leech this period of incarceration was difficult and trying, as with all the prisoners. But in many ways, he explained to the young Christian, it was just a continuation of the way he had already been living as a missionary in India, He received no fixed salary, for the RBMU was a "faith mission" which never appealed for funds. The workers simply prayed for the needs of the mission and its missionaries to be supplied. Sometimes the remittance he received was low and sometimes it was high, He and his family "lived by faith", and their needs had always been met, though sometimes funds came from the most unexpected sources. Looking back in later years to his time of captivity, Lionel was able to testify, "Through John Leech I learned to live the life of faith in God each day as it came, and I ceased to be anxious about my survival."

Haylor's major blueprint for survival in the prison camp was a strong faith in God. But second to this was the need for mental stimulation. He was aware of the need to keep his mind developed for the sake of acquiring new knowledge, as well as the importance of being distracted from his squalid surroundings and the frequent pains in his stomach which brought weakness and inactivity. A library was opened in Changi, and he frequently recorded the books which he was reading. Early in captivity lectures were organised on a wide range of subjects – Languages, Mathematics, Economics, Wood and Metal Work, Shorthand, Book-keeping and Agriculture. They were under the direction of two highly qualified officers of the Army Educational Corps.

The difficulties facing the leaders of this ambitious programme were legion – poor accommodation, lack of paper and almost no textbooks. The lecturer simply squatted in the dust and expounded on his special subject. The scheme was successful from the start in spite of the handicaps, and good attendances were maintained. Lionel made these entries in his diary –

30 Mar 1942. *Started lectures on many subjects. Am taking farming. Think some knowledge might be useful.*
3 Apr 1942. *Classes seem useful and take the mind off.*
13 Apr 1942. *Another poultry and farming lecture.*
18 Apr 1942. *University courses opened. We are getting high brow.*
6 May 1942. *Am thinking of getting Wireless lectures when poultry finishes.*

But he never had the opportunity of attending Wireless lectures, for he was to move on from Changi. But the setting up of a Changi University on 28th April was a major achievement when allowance is made for the atrocious conditions in the camp; and Lionel availed himself of its facilities both to extend his knowledge and to take his mind off the trials and tribulations of his captivity.

Then thirdly Haylor was a staunch believer in what is today called "Positive Thinking". He had the ability to flood his mind with optimistic hopes about the future, to conjure up and picture past happy events in his life in Romford, and to record in his diary his daily experiences in the most favourable light. Most important of all, as we have seen, his positive thinking was firmly linked with positive trusting. His optimism, cheerfulness and ability to see the daily events in their most favourable light were based on his personal faith in Divine Providence.

The day's entry in his diary was always cheerful and confident, although close friends had died and his own survival with perpetual dysentery and physical weakness was not a certainty. The daily entry usually closed with such phrases as "*Very good. All O.K.*"

Lionel must have known that sometimes he was hovering between life and death. But when after a heavy day's work he lay down with swollen feet and a painful stomach on his hard stone bed, he flooded his mind with thoughts of his family back at home, with treasured memories of his times with Joan and their love for each other, of the Congregational Church in South Street and its many activities, of his work and his friends at the Post Office. It was like turning over the pages of a family photograph album, stopping and pausing in front of some snaps for longer than others.

And writing up his diary was like talking to his loved ones, and doing it in this way made the hard life in Changi far more bearable. These extracts will serve to show his daily recordings of his life was in imagination an intimate conversation with those he loved across the sea -

16 Apr 1942.   *Many happy returns, darling. Hope to wish next time in person.*
29 Aug 1942.   *Feeling this past few days of being near home. May be cards reached you.*
22 Oct 1942.   *Many happy returns, Mum. With luck with you at next.*

Perhaps we could sum all this up with the words of the Te Deum Laudamus - "O Lord, in Thee have I trusted. Let me never be confounded."

Chapter 3.
Marching Orders To Go East.

(Voyage 25/10/42 - 13/11/42)

In many ways Changi was an important and strategic staging camp. Into it came bedraggled groups of soldiers and sailors captured in small and large groups after the surrender of Singapore. Out from it went thousands of "physically fit" prisoners who were transferred to Saigon to do heavy work on the docks, and to Thailand and Burma to help in the construction of the Burma road and railway.

By the end of March, 1942, six weeks after Changi Camp was opened, there were no less than 45,000 prisoners, and during the previous month there had been briefly as many as 52,200 inmates (See Appendix 1). The mind boggles at these statistics. Civilian internment camps in China were considered large if they had as many as 2,000. Changi was larger than a village, and the feeding, housing and guarding of such numbers must have proved a mammoth task to the Japanese authorities. Clearly it was advantageous to them to transfer large groups to areas where the prisoners could assist in the war effort (though the Geneva Convention forbade it), thus depleting this highly populated camp.

The movements in and out of camp were unsettling enough, and sometimes good friends bade farewell as they departed to "destination unknown". It might well be the last time Haylor would see them. But rumours of future departures were even harder to bear. Few prisoners could feel settled and secure, and the possibility of a transfer across the seas brought with it the fear that conditions there might be even worse. Lionel wrote -

> 8 May 1942. *First rumours of our movement. Many destinations suggested. No wish to go abroad. See where I'm led though.*
> 23 May 1942. *Movement orders about. Don't think it's us.*
> 16 Aug 1942. *Generals, brigadiers and colonels taken away ? to Japan.*

This went on month after month, but in October it seemed clear that Lionel would soon be leaving. During this month there was a massive programme of transfers out of Changi to Java, Japan and Formosa, totalling no less than 23,882 prisoners. Soon it became unmistakable to Lionel that his turn was coming soon -

> 23 Oct 1942. *1,100 of our area of 1,700 moving in one bunch. I'm down to go. To me it's always "God's will be done". Moving overseas - no destination.*
> 24 Oct 1942. *Did many odds and ends to go away. Said cheerio to friends. V. Good friends too.*
> 25 Oct 1942. *Moved 9 a.m. by lorry to docks. 1,100 of 11th Div. Had to wait at docks till 4 p.m. Went aboard ship. Roughly 6,000 tons. 1,100 of us and 1,000 Jap. troops. Ship "England Maru". All in holds. Sleeping space 5 ft by 1 1/2 ft by 4 ft. Jap cooking on deck. Lavs on deck v. primitive. V. hot in holds.*

And so the next stage in Lionel's life as a prisoner was now beginning. On 25th October he boarded the *England Maru*, a 6,000 ton cattle boat. She presented a sorry sight as he approached her. The sides were patched in several places - she looked as though she would disintegrate at the slightest bump. The boat had been built in 1905 on Clydeside, and had been sold by the British for scrap fourteen years previously. All kinds of jokes were to be made about her as the voyage proceeded. Submarines were known to be active in these

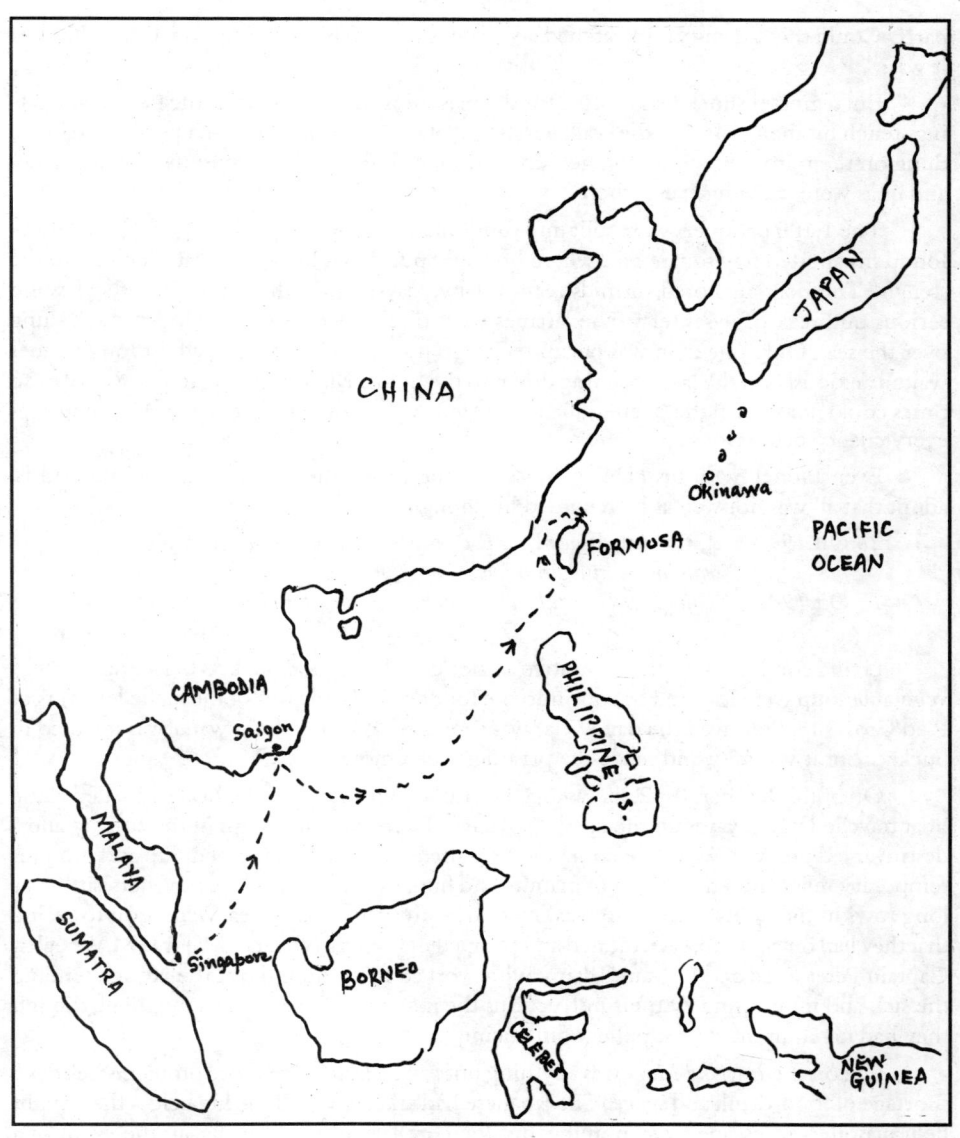

Map 1. The Voyage from Changi Camp, Singapore to Taihoku Camp, Formosa.

parts. Could this old rusty and patched vessel get them safely to their destination, wherever it was?

But a greater shock was in store for the prisoners. As they entered the boat a nauseating stench hit their nostrils - the walls and floors of the holds had the remains of dried horse dung on them from previous voyages. Everything was filthy and verminous - cockroaches and bugs were crawling everywhere.

The 1,100 prisoners were split into four holds, each tightly packed. Soon each soldier found his allotted few square feet where he could put down his kit, and sit, albeit amid the stench. The boat anchored in midstream for five days, but in that brief time there was a serious outbreak of dysentery. The latrines were on the deck, each a wooden stack slung over the sea. Only one man was permitted to go up on deck at a time, whilst long queues waited anxiously on the ladders going down to the holds. Many needing to go twenty or so times could not wait in the queues, and so the stench got worse as each day passed; there was every chance of a serious epidemic.

Even Lionel, with his habit of always trying to see the brighter side of life, had to admit that all was not well as he recorded his thoughts -

    26 Oct 1942.   ... Conditions nearly as poor as possible to be. Sweat very much. No washing, v. little drinking.
    27 Oct 1942.   Things really awful - but can't help smiling through.

Living conditions were as primitive as they could be. Food buckets of rice and watery vegetable soup were lowered by rope into the four holds. Some tins of meat, the leftovers of Red Cross supplies, saved the day. What was supposed to be drinking water was lowered in buckets; but it was salty, and made the prisoners even more thirsty

On 30th October, 1942, the voyage began, and for four days the heavily loaded cattle boat travelled northwards up the coast of Malaya. There were five ships in the convoy, and a destroyer led the way. Welcome cool breezes wafted through the cramped ship and brought temporary relief amid the stench of manure and human excrement. The travellers, sitting in long rows in the holds of the ship weak with dysentery and diarrhoea, were soon to realise that they had on board three dedicated and competent medical officers - Major B.M.Wheeler, Captain Peter Seed and Captain Blair - who worked hard throughout the voyage tending the sick and minimising by their instructions the many health hazards facing them, though they had no equipment or supplies of medicine.

Life on the *England Maru* was anything but easy. There were more problems besides a shortage of food, drink and space. The Japanese had taken away all the life belts - they might help prisoners to escape by swimming; but the corollary of this was that in the event of a shipwreck or being torpedoed they stood no chance of survival. Then music and singing had been forbidden - this was one way by which they could have kept their spirits up in these appalling surroundings. They could go up on deck in relays for very short periods. When they did do so they took in deep breaths of fresh air and scanned the horizon, before squashing up in the hold once again and counting the hours till the next trip on deck was due.

Lionel put down his own thoughts -
    31 Oct 1942.   *Jogging along. Fair. Sweat lot still ... Tom P. holds services of prayer*

                    each evening.
1 Nov 1942.   *Boat trying to stand on end. Tummy feeling effect. Small service in evening. Had to be on back quite a bit. O.K.*

These brief informal times of prayer with fellow Christians lifted him up above the sickening stench and the severely tight living conditions of the cattle boat. He lay on his blanket and recalled St. Paul's hazardous voyage to Rome, also as a prisoner. The apostle's confident faith amid the dangers inspired his fellow travellers. That was surely his task as a Christian on this terrible voyage.

On 3rd November the boat dropped anchor off Saigon. But in the afternoon she travelled on, first southwards and then eastwards before turning north. The sea was now rougher and the many hazards to health – of inadequate diet, the overpowering stench, the stuffiness, lack of washing facilities – were having their effects on the hundreds of prisoners. Among the troops there was dysentery, diptheria, typhoid and prickly heat. Rain was pouring into the holds and the prisoners' clothes were turning mouldy – Lionel had both a stomach trouble and a bad cold. The medical officers were bravely doing their best to limit the disease and illness on ship, though without any medical supplies.

Here are some extracts from Haylor's diary –

5 Nov 1942.   *Tummy a bit queer.*
8 Nov 1942.   *Me on back. Just manage to eat and keep it down.*
9 Nov 1942.   *Feeling poorly.*
11 Nov 1942. *Oh deary me, what a tum I've got... Able to eat a little ... Two lads very poorly, another nearly died.*
12 Nov 1942. *One of chaps died at 9.30 p.m.*

Soon it became clear that Formosa was their destination. The boat anchored briefly on 12th November to the south of the island, and then sailed north up the coast to the west of the island. On 14th November they reached Keelung on the north eastern tip of Formosa. Amid heavy rain they disembarked at 8.30 a.m. Drenched to the skin and desperately hungry, they were lined up on the wharf and counted. The local populace looked on, obviously distressed at the physical condition of the Western prisoners. They were then marched to the railway station, and sat in train carriages with the wooden shutters closed down tightly. They were half an hour on the train. Lionel describes what happened next –

14 Nov 1942. *...Wet through and cold. All the town out to meet us. Eats - a kind of rice and barley cake. March 2 to 3 miles. Children and people lined street. Some of kids looked sweet. Most people looked sad. Place very civilized, but looks very militarised.*

They were now coming to their next prison camp – Taihoku on the north west coast of Formosa. Standing in the cold, wet wind they were ordered to strip. They were searched and then sprayed with disinfectant. All their kit was taken, but somehow the diary was preserved. They put on their wet clothes again, and were issued with a towel, some soap and a pair of wooden clogs, a sheet and blankets, a bowl and a fork. Most welcome of all was a meal of meat, rice and vegetable stew.

As they walked through the camp to the huts allotted to them and carrying their new kit, Japanese and Formosan guards with fixed bayonets could be seen on duty everywhere. Eighty men were crowded into each of these primitive prison huts which were made of mud and bamboo. These huts gave them little protection from wind, rain and cold. Tired from the journey the prisoners went to bed at 10 p.m. and fell asleep in their new surroundings. After that three week voyage in the cattle boat, at least they could now breathe in a clean air, wash themselves down and hope for better days.

But they were to be no less than two and three quarters years in Formosa, and to face problems they had never known in Changi or on the *England Maru*.

Chapter 4.
The Rigours of Taihoku Camp, Formosa.

(Period: 14/11/42 – 11/11/43)

For the 600 prisoners incarcerated in Taihoku Camp life was quite different from that in Changi. In the summer there was sunshine and gentle breezes from the sea, but in winter it could be bitterly cold, and they had insufficient clothing and blankets to keep them warm. Not far from the camp were valleys growing fruit in abundance, and so either on the menu or purchased at the canteen small amounts of tomatoes, apples, oranges and, more frequently, bananas could be obtained.

But the new life was very regimented. Upon arrival each prisoner was finger-printed, given a number to wear and was photographed. When passing a guard the prisoner was expected to jump to attention and bow, and any movement which was deemed half hearted or inadequate earned a slap or a punch; and sometimes the guard hid round a corner and jumped out unexpectedly, and applied these humiliating punishments if the prisoner did not react quickly enough. Major Ben Wheeler, the camp doctor, wrote in his diary of 1st March, 1943, "*Yesterday one of the sentries at the corner of the hospital spent most of the morning slapping or striking people whose bow did not please him - no love taps either, as he knocked a tooth out of one.*" Every three weeks there was a change of guards, and so it was necessary to know the foibles and whims of the new batch, and to identify which guard was prone to roughness or violence.

Haylor recorded -

16 Nov 1942. Learning orders and numbers in Japanese.

It was certainly in his interest to be able to number off in Japanese and to know some basic Japanese. Counting went as follows -

Ichi, ni, san, shi, go, roku, shichi, hachi, kyu, ju.

He might know his normal number, but if some colleague was absent at Rollcall it was essential to be able to jump from number 157 to 156.

Then there were the instructions which they received daily at the Rollcall -

> kyotskee - stand at attention
> yasumay - stand at ease
> bango - number off

And if he was out on the road working the guard might shout out some of the following -

> hyaku - hurry up
> nani suru ka? - what are you doing?
> bakeroo - stupid (it was actually swearing)

The day's programme was tightly planned. At 6.30 a.m. the bugle awoke them. The prisoner had to quickly wash himself, shave, dress and tidy his bed. At 7.00 a.m. came Rollcall and with it the need to number off in Japanese, to salute the officer twice and the Imperial Palace. At 7.30 a.m. was breakfast - normally rice and barley, green-boiled leaves as tea, and vegetables. At 8.0 a.m. they went out in their working parties. Lionel's work included pushing trucks, working on a railway line and filling in sunken roadways. At 12.30 p.m. there was lunch, which was similar to breakfast, and at 1.30 p.m. they were back to their manual work. Supper was at 6.00 p.m. and Rollcall again at 6.30 p.m.; and lights were out at 8.30 p.m.

On the 22nd January, 1943, Lionel had an accident in which a shovel badly cut three fingers on his right hand. In these conditions nothing healed rapidly and cuts could easily turn septic, but for several months he nursed the fingers with care. Being ambidextrous he wrote his diary now with his left hand and the records were clear and legible. He was given lighter work to do for some weeks.

Two months after the incident he wrote in his diary -

17 Mar 1943.   *Had hand cleaned up. Not too bad. Only got small dressing on top of fingers. Can't use fingers cos they're too stiff. Dr. put me on antibiotics now. Told me to use fingers as much as possible.*
26 Mar 1943.   *Middle finger now uncovered. Only lost little bit. Nail not grown much.*

Six weeks after Lionel Haylor arrived at Taihoku Camp it was Christmas Day. He described it as *"a day of big surprises"*. He worked until 11 a.m. and then the prisoners were given the remainder of the day off.

25 Dec 1942.   *In the afternoon 120 lbs of flour and 4 pigs taken into cookhouse. Two Jap. cooks recruited to prepare tea. Carol service at 3.30 p.m. Very nice. Sang more outside our hospital. Our tea - what a shaking - 6 oz. pork grilled in batter. Thick veg. stew and extra rice. Sweet tea. Was definitely a God-send. Made Xmas Day seem real. Very grateful. Thinking of you very much, and hope your Xmas was nice too. Hope may be with you at the next. God bless.*

A week later came a festival to which the Japanese attached more significance - New Year. No work was done. There was a brief parade which included pausing to pay respects to the Emperor. The meals were good. Lionel's diary records that for breakfast each prisoner had eight bananas (doubtless he saved some) and a piece of *"festival cake"*; for dinner three bananas and *"pork stew with small flapjack at tea"*. He described it as a *"nice quiet day"*.

But they were soon back to the rigid regimentation, inadequate meals and heavy manual work. They were called out of bed for Rollcall twice a night. Haylor's diary which previously summed up his condition as *"doing O.K."* now frequently uses the word *"fair"*, which with his tendency to play down his problems probably meant "poor".

3 Jan 1943.   *Fair meals.*
4 Jan   *Fair day.*
5 Jan   *Felt tired to-day.*
7 Jan   *Food fair.*
11 Jan   *Cold at night. Slept cold.*
17 Jan   *Weighed 55 kgm. Am thin, but am doing O.K.*
18 Jan   *Told not to complain about food - best being done for us*

The first three months of 1943 were difficult in every way. The small camp hospital, an army hut, was jammed with prisoners struggling with disease and malnutrition. Some were losing sensation in their hands and feet due to vitamin deficiency. Others were experiencing intense burning of the feet at night. The most common sicknesses were diptheria and famine oedema. The authorities had little sympathy with prisoners who were in hospital and off work. Sometimes they dragged them out and put them through stiff physical exercises which were far beyond their strength, and some collapsed. Because some prisoners were too weak to work they cut their rice rations by a third, but later they reversed this. The diary stated –

22 Mar 1943. *Mess now decided not to cut sick rations.*
23 Mar 1943. *180 cases of beri beri so far, and on increase daily. 10 bags of polished rice came in gateway. Might help a little. Things otherwise going fairly.*
24 Mar 1943. *All beri beri cases now getting some extra treatment.*

Lionel realised that in the battle for survival he needed spiritual strength and Christian fellowship. He was keeping up his daily Bible readings and recording the passage he read in his diary - sometimes half a chapter, but more often three chapters. He attended the Sunday services - a typical entry for Sunday would be "*Fair day. Two good services*". But it is noticeable that he records no deep conversations (or "*jaws*" as he calls them) with fellow Christians such as he had had at Changi - with men like John Leech who had been a tower of strength in those difficult times.

But he was still maintaining prayer and Bible reading –

21 Mar 1943. *Started making a small hymn book.*
22 Mar 1943. *Hoping may be to have small prayer meeting soon.*
31 Mar 1943. *Have completed reading the Bible from cover to cover. 298 days. Not too bad for me. Am just a little homesick.*

John Leech had taught him to live "the life of faith" a day at a time. At this low point his needs were going to be supplied once again. April brought some pleasant surprises –

1 Apr 1943. *Fool's day, but we haven't been fooled. Good news. Told that Red Cross supplies - food, clothing and medicine - on the island. Expect in camp any time to a fortnight.*

Camp rumours could be hurtful and leave the prisoners low with disappointment. But there was a ring of truth about this one. In the first week of April ten lorry loads came trundling into Taihoku Camp; and the Japanese seemed to have become more flexible and reasonable. Instead of handling the parcels themselves and issuing the food as and when they felt like it, this batch was placed directly in the hands of the prisoners' own Supply Officer. As the parcels were opened the guards expressed surprise at their contents. How could Britain, a defeated nation, provide such food for their prisoners of war?

For the kitchen supplies the Red Cross had sent bully beef, M&V., sugar, salt, aspirins and boots. In the individual parcels there was sugar, cheese, bacon, syrup, tomato, margarine, Nestlé milk, meat rolls, cream rice, beef vegetable, chocolate, tea, soup, fruit pudding and biscuits.

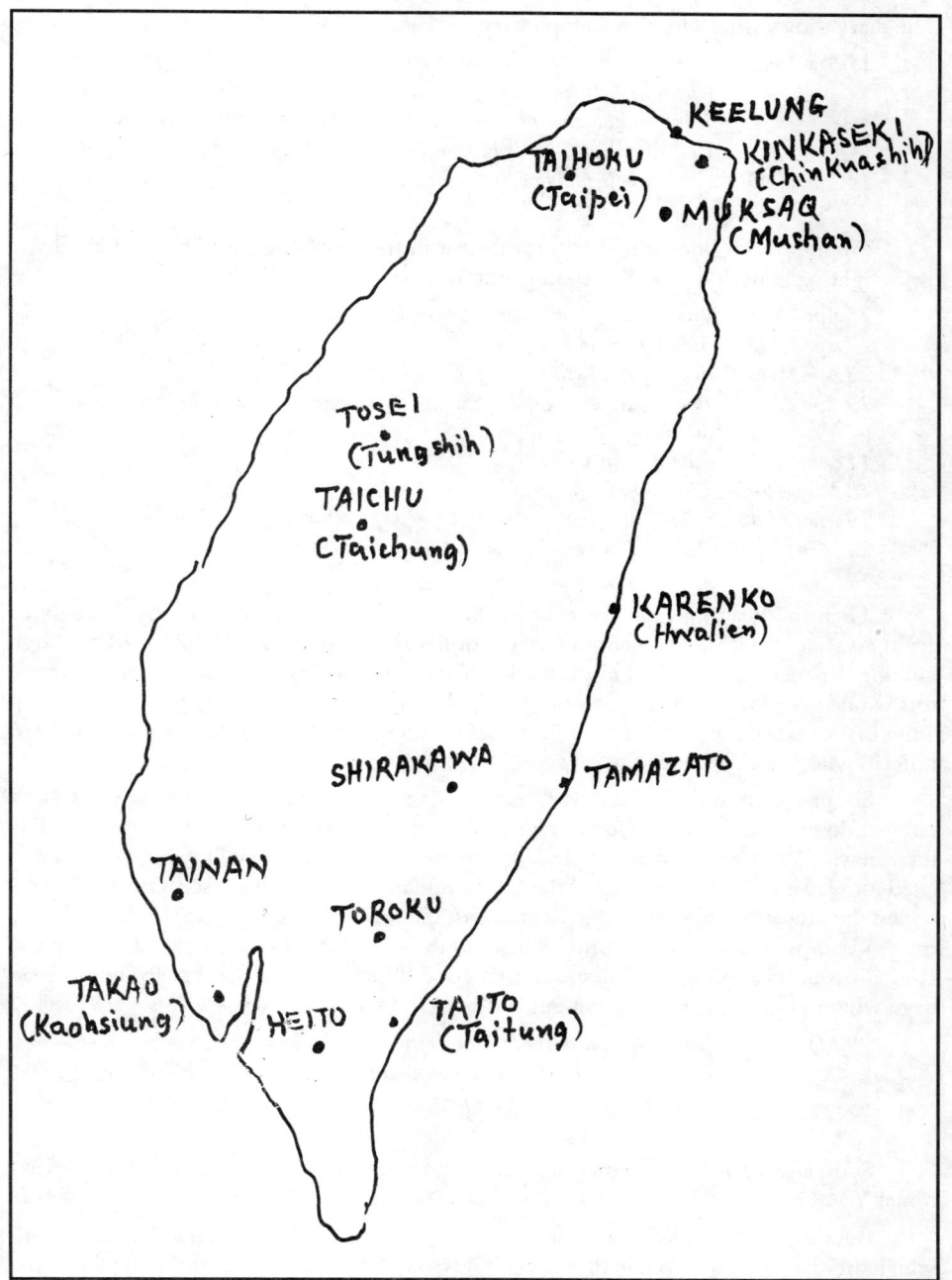

Map 2. *Japanese P.O.W. Camps in Formosa.*
(Present names of places are put in brackets, where different.)

The diary shows what a lift these supplies gave the young P.O.W. –

> 11 Apr 1943   What a grand day. The issue of parcels. I've never felt so good for a long time. Mine was sent from Bermondsey British Red Cross and St. John's Ambulance on Apr. 16, 1942. Had two lovely services and really thanked God for His goodness to us. Went to bed absolutely full.
>
> 14 Apr 1943. Ate a whole pudding, but pain after.

In spite of this boost the diary reveals that in the weeks which followed Lionel was again fighting ill health, though making light of it.

> 25 Apr 1943   Tummy very troublesome, but easier by night time.
> 27 Apr 1943   Tummy not so bad.
> 28 Apr 1943   Tummy not right yet, but taking it easy.
> 29 Apr 1943   Bad night. Bronchial tubes puffing. Don't like it. Hope it will ease down.
> 11 May 1943   Chest about O.K.
> 18 May 1943   Bit wheezy.
> 19 May 1943   Chest still wheezy.
> 28 May 1943   Rain. Got wet. Brought on wheezy chest.

Then the health problem is eclipsed by another welcome event in the camp, once again associated with that splendid organisation – the Red Cross. On 27th May a high ranking Japanese General had inspected them, no doubt to ensure that the imminent visitors would get a favourable impression. On 29th May three cars drew up at Taihoku Camp – the first one had Japanese officers in it, and in the second and third were three Western officials who proved to be Swiss.

Six prisoners were interviewed, representing a cross section of the camp – from a colonel down to those in the lower ranks. The Japanese Commandant was present. The interviews could have been conducted quickly in English, but everything had to be translated into Japanese. The presence of the Commandant inhibited free discussion, but nevertheless the visitors must have gauged the fact that the prisoners were in poor health and were carrying out manual labour beyond their strength. The visit boosted camp morale, for the Red Cross officials informed the group that good things were on the way to them – mail bags, winter clothing, sports equipment and books. Lionel observed –

> 29 May 1943. Seems that we are at last under the Red Cross eye. Believe the chap is to remain on the island. He is middle aged and white. Hopes are up lots. Had 4 or 5 potatoes for tea.

Soon afterwards some games, an accordion and 200 books arrived from the International Y.M.C.A.

But there were trials of every kind after this period of encouragement. The 25 pounds which they had each received in their parcels was soon eaten up; and the extra supplies in the kitchen when spread over 600 men had not lasted long. There were earthquakes on the island which undid some of the backbreaking work they had been doing on the roads; there was subsidence, and the ground had to be levelled off again to be fit for heavy lorries. Camp guards had been moved on to serve in the war, and those left behind, stretched to the limit, were barking out their orders gruffly. Then in July came torrential rains and high winds which kept the prisoners awake at night and badly damaged the fragile huts.

> 18 July 1943.   Rain like old harry. Water rose about 9 feet. Flooded the camp waist deep. We evacuated in afternoon with kit, wading waist deep. Water subsided before night - managed to get back to hut. Scene of desolation in camp. Fence down, huts with walls down. Lost ducks and one pig escaped. First meal for 24 hrs. Things now wet and mucky but will dry.
>
> 19 July 1943.   Clearing up. All water subsided. Camp looks a wreck ... more rain in evening.

What little order and comfort they had built up since their arrival in the Taihoku Camp was gone in one swoop. The chimneys had toppled and there were big gaping holes in the bungalows. There was much repair work to be done, and they had little resources and limited strength to tackle this task.

The arrivals and departures of prisoners were unsettling experiences in these circumstances where friendships and personal relationships were so important for morale. The coming of new faces required having to adjust to different types of people, and those who left were keenly missed. On 25th June some generals were taken away, probably to go to Japan; on 19th August 40 officers departed ... and so it went on. The most poignant was the departure of "Bill" on 9th August -

> 9 Aug 1943.   Big surprise. 120 men called out for a move. Bill in it. Not me. Move to another camp in Taiwan. Very sorry that Bill and I being split. Still am alive and kicking, so keep chin up.
>
> 10 Aug 1943.   Very much in the dumps. Chaps left by train 7 a.m. Didn't care much for Bill to go. Very lonely afterwards. Felt better by night. Chaps arrived new camp 2 p.m.

Behind those terse details lies the story of 120 men marching out of camp to the station, a brief train ride and then a difficult climb with their kit up a rough rocky road. The men, already weak, stumbled and fell, but were forced by their guards to get up and continue. Ten men died as a result of this march. Taihoku Camp had been bad, but Kinkaseki Camp to which they went was the "Hell Camp of Formosa". It was perched on a rocky hillside. The prisoners slept on bare boards in closely packed wooden huts. Lice and bedbugs were everywhere. Those who were considered "fit" had to daily climb down the 1,730 uneven rough hewn steps into the copper mine. There were injuries from accidents as well as sickness from diseases.

Back at the Taihoku Camp Lionel Haylor's time was taken up with repairing the damage from the flooding, and helping in the building of an oven in the kitchen. His diary shows that the need for greens in their diet was becoming the overriding priority -

> 31 Aug 1943.   Big veg. issue. Seem to be giving us veg.
>
> 3 Sept.   Back to turnips and green stuff for veg.
>
> 8 Sept.   Quite a lot of boils and festers about, due to lack of green veg. Green

>   *veg. coming in now.*
>
> *18 Sept.*   *Huts being repaired by coolies. For winter I suppose.*

Life in camp was a series of ups and downs. The prisoners were like the soldiers of the Grand Old Duke of York -

And when they were up, they were up,
And when they were down, they were down,
And when they were only half way up,
They were neither up nor down.

In September it seemed that the outside world was taking notice of them again. On 21st September the camp was cleaned up for further visitors, and on the following day they were sent out to do different work, well out of sight of any officials who might come. On 23rd September a "Neutral Delegation", consisting of a Swiss and a Swedish official, made a tour of the camp. But the squalid conditions were there for all to see. Even the briefest tour of Taihoku Camp could not conceal that. Lionel observes -

> *23 Sept. 1943*   *We are definitely under the notice of someone now. So that's to the good.*

But this visit was followed by decreased rations.

> *29 Sept 1943*   *Decrease in rations. Things not so bad.*
> *30 Sept.*   *Veg. very small issue.*
> *1 Oct.*   *Good curry stew at tea.*

On that same day his daily Bible reading gave him courage.

Jesus said unto him, "If thou canst believe, all things are possible to him that believeth"; and the father said with tears, "Lord, I believe, help Thou my unbelief." (Mark 9 vv. 23, 24)

Lionel remarks, "*Very encouraging piece in to-day's Bible reading.*" He knew that in this primitive camp with its problems of hunger, sickness and many uncertainties his faith had wavered. He repeated under his breath, "*Lord, I do trust you. Sorry for having doubted you.*"

He was working long hours with a team of prisoners who were planting 5,000 cabbage plants. He could not help wondering whether he and his colleagues would themselves benefit from this programme to grow food for the camp. On 10th November Haylor was ordered to a work parade, and was told that he was one of a party of 50 men who would be moving to another camp. The Japanese officer painted a glowing picture of their new camp home. It enjoyed a good climate, the food would be more plentiful and the working conditions were less heavy. Their kit was searched, and they stood waiting for further orders. Lionel wrote -

> *10 Nov 1943*   *The best day I've had here. Moving 9 a.m. to-morrow.*

The atmosphere surrounding their departure the next morning was surprisingly relaxed compared with past moves; and the guards seemed to be treating them better than usual. As the lorries carried the 50 men to the station they waved good-bye to their friends left behind. Lionel remarked, "*Authorities being lenient in letting us say cheerio to pals*", and he added sadly, "*Leaving Ron. P. behind.*" The train journey was comfortable, and the prisoner described it as "*a most delightful journey, going about 120 miles south. Beautiful scenery.*" They left the train at 4 p.m., and then had a half hour journey by lorry.

They entered Taichu Camp in the centre of Formosa. There were 375 British prisoners already there, and they appeared to be in a fit condition. Their settling in went smoothly – their belongings were checked, and they were assigned to their huts. A surprisingly pleasant and adequate meal was set before them, and they were assured by their new colleagues that this was a typical meal. Before dropping off to a heavy peaceful sleep, Haylor wrote –

11 Nov 1943   The next best, if not best, day I've had.

So this is Taichu Camp.

Photograph of Lionel Haylor taken in 1940,
before being stationed abroad.

Life in Taiwan Camps

Cattle raising in the P.O.W. Camp

Rest day in the Camp.

Prisoners of war receive a visit from the International Red Cross - June 1944

Photos: F.E.P.O. Journal, Aug. 1945.

Life in Taiwan Camps

Australian, American and British Officers being interviewed by I.R.C. delegates

Sweet potato harvest at Taihoku Camp

Prisoners looking after pigs

Photos: F.E.P.O. Journal, Aug. 1945.

Life in Taiwan Camps

Japanese guards with delegate from the I.R.C. June 1944
Photo: F.E.P.O. Journal, Aug. 1945.

When the Japanese retreat began the "situation map" in each camp fell behind the events

Photo: J. Edwards in "Banzai you Bastards".

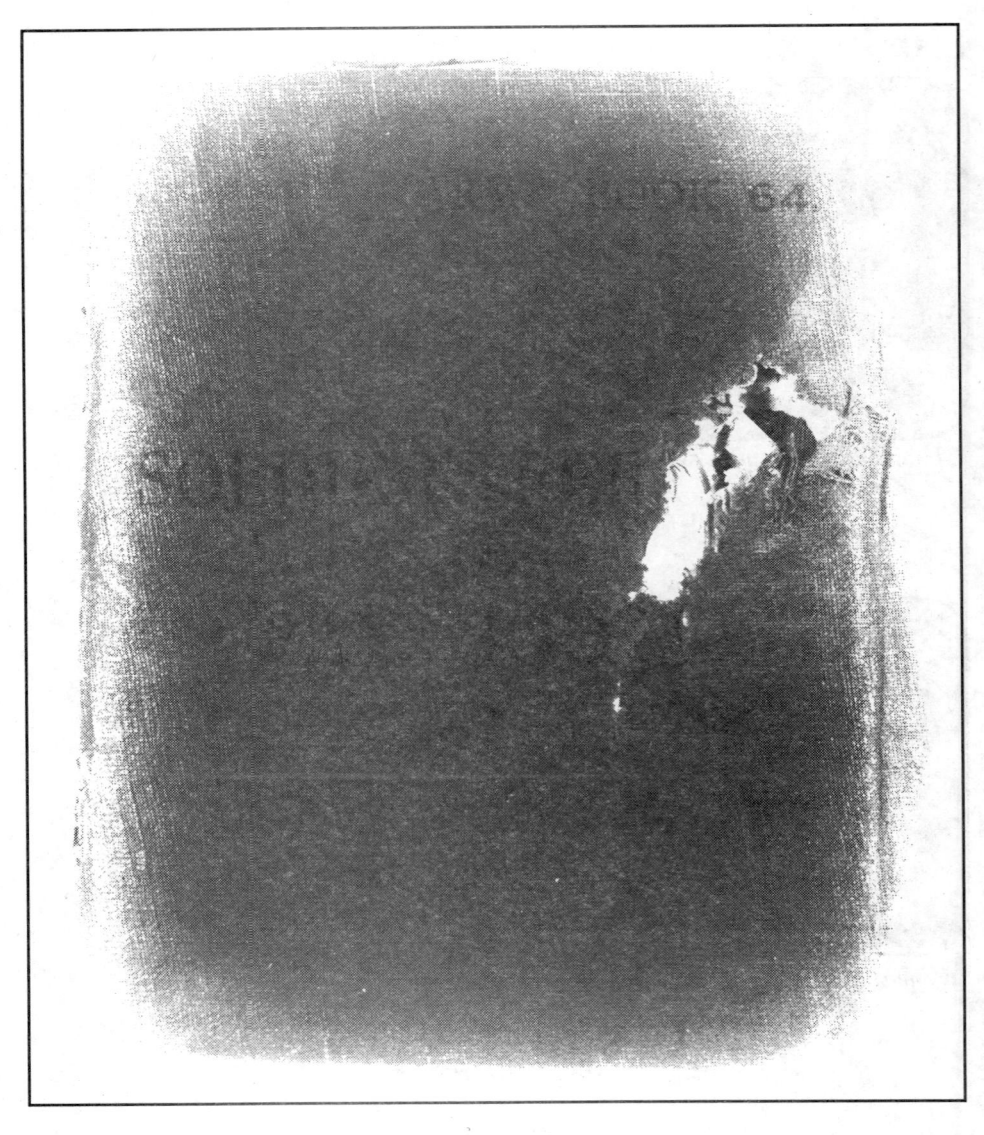

Cover of Soldiers Service and Pay book - with bullet hole

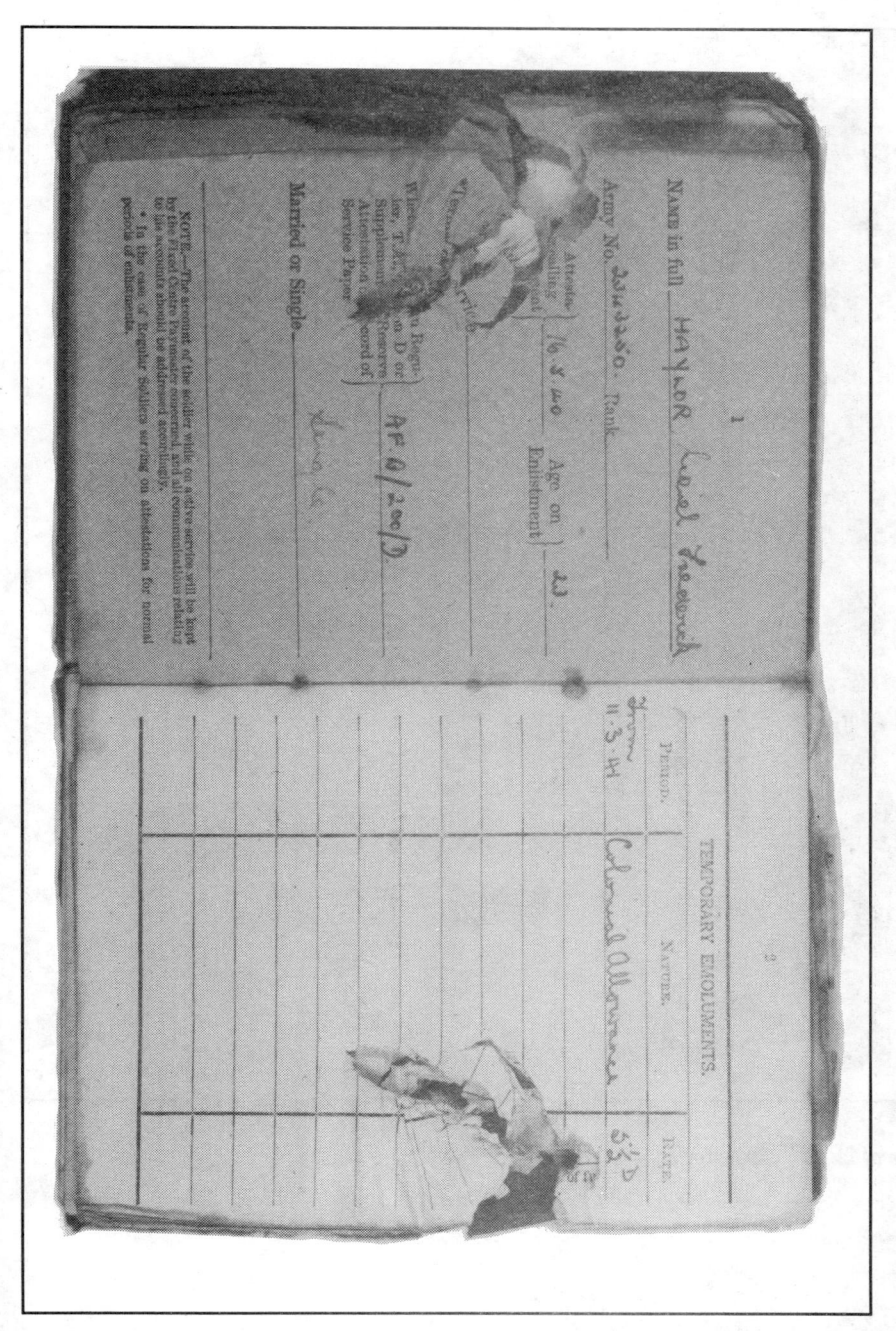

Inside spread of Lionel Haylor's Soldier's Pay Book, showing bullet hole

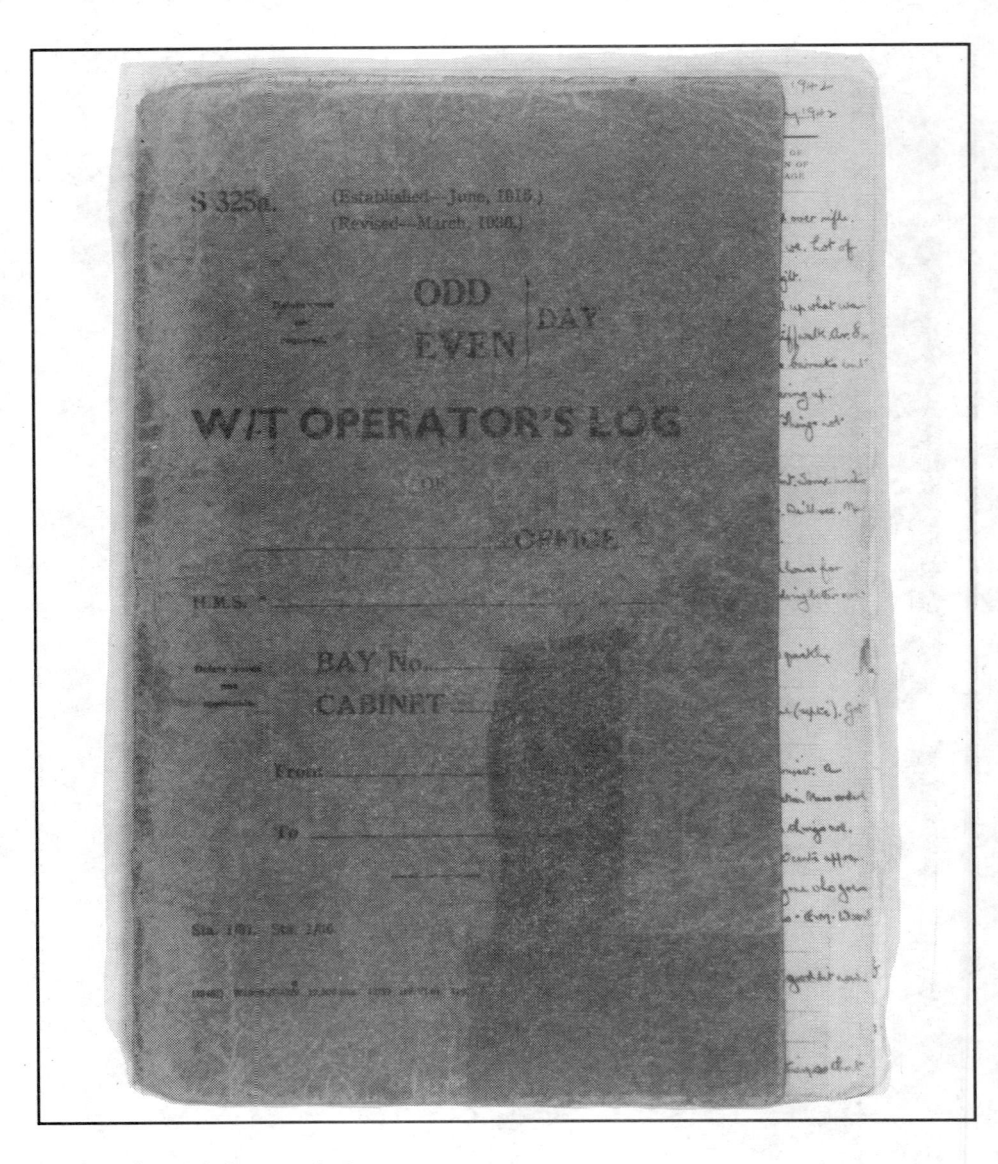

Cover of W/T Operator's Log

Pages of Lionel Haylor's Allowance Book

Chapter 5.
Taichu Camp
and the Arrival of Mail from Home.

(Period 12/11/43 to 28/6/44)

There was every indication that life would be more bearable for the prisoners in Taichu. Lionel had come here in poor health, and his first impressions were such that he expressed the hope that *"food and conditions here will pull us up."* Watering gardens, weeding and digging was not such heavy work as he had been doing, though later this was to change. Then he noted that regulations were *"easier"*. The regimentation of Taihoku Camp was thankfully now a thing of the past. The huts too were a little more comfortable. And, last but not least, the scenic outlook from the Taichu Camp was inspiring. The prisoners could look at the snow-capped mountains in the distance, a much needed reminder that, though they were living in unhygienic conditions, outside was the beautiful world which God had created.

Lionel Haylor wrote –

18 Nov 1943.   *Things will be much better here. Looking forward to completing P.O.W. time in these better conditions.*

22 Nov 1943.   *Hot bath here every other night. Huts have decent windows and doors, but thatched roofs. Things generally very good.*

31 Dec 1943.   *Things definitely on up grade. Personally here feel stronger, more energetic.*

Within a few weeks of arrival the manual work became heavier. The prisoners were employed in riverbed construction, and in effect had to do the work of a mechanical digger, each man lifting and pushing two tons of rock per day on to trucks.

1 Dec 1943.   *Out working on the proper job. Stones. Heavy work. Think I can make it O.K. Dinner is brought to us. Very like picnicking.*

With the increasing shortage of food on the island the prisoners had to take their turn planting acres and acres of peanuts and potatoes. It would be some time before there would be fruit for their hard work, but most of it would go to feed the Japanese military personnel on the island.

Christmas 1943 came, and his first and only Christmas at Taichu he described as the best since becoming a P.O.W., *"in fact the best since 1939"*. After breakfast the inmates were each issued with two small loaves, two cakes and two parcels of caramels. Then they had a carol service. Some were wiping their eyes while singing – they were remembering earlier Christmases back in England – the decorations, the gifts and children's laughter. For dinner they had bread in the place of the usual rice, then thick pork stew, bananas and tomatoes. In the afternoon some of their number produced "Cinderella" – however did they get those colourful costumes? A Christmas message from the Red Cross was read to them. Everyone was happy, and for a few brief hours the prisoners' spirits were lifted by these make-shift celebrations.

25 Dec 1943.   *Altogether the best day yet. God is indeed good to us. Here's hoping we might be worthy of it.*

The New Year too was full of revelry. There was the special parade in the morning at which respects were formally shown to the Emperor. There was a good stew for dinner, and then a concert in the afternoon. This was interrupted by an air raid warning and then resumed. Amid much hilarity they sang Auld Lang Syne.

> *1 Jan 1944. All of us sang ourselves hoarse. Was good, and didn't seem a bit like a P.O.W. camp.*

Early in 1944 the manual work was getting heavier, and the prisoners' health, after two years of captivity, was clearly deteriorating. They struggled through their manual work, and more of the men were succumbing to the diseases caused by vitamin deficiency.

> *5 Feb 1944. Doctor says got beri beri. Getting powder for it.*

But a pleasant surprise temporarily took Lionel's mind off his physical condition. "*As cold waters to a thirsty soul, so is good news from a far country.*" (Proverbs 25 v. 25). The 28th March, 1944, was a day of great rejoicing. After two years of imprisonment he at last heard from home. Back in Taihoku days, on 18th February, 1943, some mail had arrived from Britain, which had been posted in July, 1942, seven months previously. But of the fifteen letters none had been for him. Three days later he had recorded in his diary that his family must now be aware of his having been captured –

> *21 Feb 1943. The P.O.W. names at Singapore printed in newspapers 2nd and 3rd July, 1942. Bet you had a worried scramble through that paper.*

Also, while at Taihoku Camp another batch of mail had arrived, and again none for Lionel.

> *5 Oct 1943. 44 letters arrived, posted May, 1943. Not for me yet. You seem to know we are here.*

Two months after his arrival in Taichu Camp a small batch of letters had arrived, and again he had been disappointed –

> *1 Jan 1944. Issue of 25 letters. All from people abroad. Nothing for me yet.*

It is impossible to realise what it must have been like to see his colleagues on all these occasions eagerly reading their letters from home, and not having any himself. But at last Lionel Haylor's turn came –

> *28 Mar 1944. GREAT NEWS. Two letters from you, my darling. Was I bucked. Posted 8/2/43 and 2/3/43. God is indeed good. There are lots more somewhere, cos you seem to be writing each Sunday. Was very excited.*

These two welcome letters had taken a year to reach him; but he read them and re-read them. More welcome mail was soon to follow –

> *17 Apr 1944. Great cheers. Two more letters and two postcards. Very pleased to have one with your writing, Mum. News very gratifying.*
>
> *25 Apr 1944. Issue of 80 letters. Grand. Me got 6. 3 from Joan - 1/8/42, 14/8/42, 23/12/42. From Mum - 19/7/42, 27/7/42 and 4/8/42.*

The letters had taken nearly two years to reach him. They represented a one-way communication, for the prisoners at that stage could not write letters back.

> *26 Apr 1944. We've never been allowed to write a letter. I haven't sent a postcard since Dec. 1943.*

But a change in this respect soon came –

> *3 May 1944. Can write letter to you 300 words. Food, war, politics taboo.*
> *7 May 1944. Sent first letter. Hoping for a swift arrival.*

While still at Taichu Camp Lionel was to receive more welcome letters – 19 on 25th May, 4 on 3rd June, 15 on 5th June, 4 on 13th June and 13 on 26th June. Also on 28th May he was allowed to write his second letter home. The uplift which this correspondence brought to him in his weakened state can only be imagined.

The prisoners when transferring from Taihoku Camp had come to Taichu full of hopes that a happier chapter lay in store for them in the new camp. Lionel had expressed the hope that he would be able to remain here for the remainder of his captivity. But six months after their arrival a heavy downpour of rain swamped the camp, and necessitated an urgent evacuation of it. The stone wall between the camp and the river was beginning to collapse, and the frail huts of the prisoners were in danger of sinking slowly into the water.

In this emergency the inmates were moved to a school in a village two miles away. Haylor, who had welcomed settling into Taichu, does not now wish to return.

> *9 Jun 1944. Hoping that camp becomes untenable, and we can't go back.*
> *11 Jun 1944. Camp being stripped. Doesn't seem as if we're going back.*
> *14 Jun 1944. Work in morning. Cleaning camp.*

On 28th June, 1944, he was one of 111 prisoners who were moved away from Taichu. A train journey of 7¼ hours took the prisoners to Takao Camp in the south of Formosa. The new camp was situated in the middle of a sugar plantation. Here Lionel was pleased to meet up with friends he had known in the earlier camps. And in this camp there were also American and Dutch prisoners.

The Taichu Camp which he had left behind would be remembered as a place where, under a reasonable Commandant and some peaceable Japanese and Formosan guards, the atmosphere had been relaxed. There had been no outbreaks of violence or other unpleasant incidents. It was also the camp where in the winter months the prisoners could look out from their sordid environment on a panoramic scene of mountains draped in snow.

The major problem here had been food, but then by now this was a problem everywhere in Formosa, both for the Japanese troops and the local populace. Formosa had become increasingly isolated due to the developments in the war in the Pacific, and in this isolation food could not be imported.

Chapter 6.
Takao Camp
and the Progress of the War.

(Period 29/6/44 to 11/3/45)

Following the raid on Pearl Harbor, Japan had made a series of swift and successful attacks, and won a ring of bases in South East Asia. The Doolittle raid on Japanese cities in April, 1942, had been the one bright spot amid a series of Allied defeats.

The initial rapid Japanese advance received a check in mid-1942, and by 1943 the Americans were pushing forward and reclaiming earlier lost ground. By the time Lionel Haylor and his fellow prisoners reached Takao Camp the war in the Pacific had reached a significant stage. The Americans and Australians had reached the Marshall Islands, the Carolines and New Guinea; and soon afterwards General Douglas MacArthur landed in the Philippines, and was to recapture Manila early in 1945.

It was a massive game of chess, and the Japanese were nervously trying to anticipate the next Allied move in their island-hopping strategy. Surely their next hop would be to Formosa. This possibility was carefully considered by the Japanese military leaders on the island, and the outcome was the sending of firm instructions to all the Commandants of P.O.W. camps that in the event of an American invasion of Formosa all prisoners were to be massacred. (See Appendix 3). This was a desperate decision and it had far-reaching implications for thousands of Allied prisoners.

Fortunately this frightening plot reached leaders in the camps through friendly Formosan guards. Had this news reached all the rank and file prisoners there might have been pandemonium, Sworn to total secrecy each group met regularly to monitor the situation, and to be one step ahead of such an eventuality.

Inmates of the camps were kept surprisingly well informed of the events of World War II, even though it might be after a delay of some weeks. Some survivors of ships torpedoed by American submarines arrived at Takao Camp with stories of atrocities and a high death rate among prisoners on the Burma railway; others came with news of the successes of American air raids on islands south of Formosa. Prisoners arriving from other camps invariably brought fresh instalments of news and/or rumours. Friendly Formosan guards would sometimes pass on recent news of the war.

But the main source of information came from Japanese-controlled newspapers in English, which were passed on by the Commandant some six weeks old. These papers were reasonably accurate about the progress of the war in Europe, but intentionally vague about the Pacific war. But the advance of the Allies in the Far East could not be concealed. The very fact that naval and air battles were taking place in the Philippines and Mariana Islands was an admission that the Allies had reached them. In the administration office in each camp was a large map of the world with Japanese flags pinned on them to show the progress of the war, but by the end of 1944 the flags were strangely lagging behind the actual events.

The prisoners on their part had to avoid appearing to look cocky or confident about the outcome of the war. In one Formosan camp the Commandant called the leaders together and gave them a lecture on how, under the spirit of Bushido and Samurai, the war could go on for a further hundred years, as all Japanese would fight to the last man. Thus their present way of life as prisoners would continue for a long time.

In October, 1944, four months after Lionel's arrival in the new camp, the war came very close to Takao with the commencement of American raids in the vicinity. On 15th, 16th and 17th October the sirens sounded, and the prisoners had to leave their work and stay in their barracks. While explosions could be heard from not far away, Japanese guards were shouting at the inmates to close all windows and doors, and *"Not to look or you will be shot"*.

Formosa had been ceded to Japan by China in 1895 after the Sino-Japanese War. By World War II the island had been developed by Japan not only economically, but also as an important naval and air base. Around Takao there were numerous airfields. The island had been used by Japan as a launch pad three years previously for the invasion of the Philippines and Indo-China; and it had played an important part as a staging point in the southward movement of troops, ships and material. Vessels and submarines had refuelled in its harbours.

Now that the Allies were on the initiative in the Pacific and moving northwards towards Japan, their planes had begun a programme of wiping out Japan's airfields and military installations on Formosa. In the months following the first raids in October, 1944, factories, dams, communications and transportation facilities were to be destroyed in further bombings.

These developments were welcome news to the prisoners languishing in Formosan camps. They were physically exhausted from nearly three years of imprisonment. They had struggled to survive on a starvation diet, though many of their comrades had died. Many had been brutally treated, and the commencement of raids, though welcome, might bring recriminations. They were doing backbreaking work for long hours and with diminishing food rations. Air raids and downpours of rain served to give them a welcome respite from their hard labour. There was sickness, mental depression and deaths in the camps; and the prisoners were dragging themselves to and from work. The closing months of 1944 and the opening months of 1945 were a critical period for them.

At Takao Camp the prisoners had a wild and unpredictable little man as their Commandant. He had a nasty temper, and kept stamping his feet and waving his Samurai sword at the slightest provocation. Earlier Christmases in the camps had been celebrated with happiness and hilarity - the manual work was reduced, there had been carol singing and concerts, and a time of goodwill with their guards.

But Christmas 1944 was quite different -

25 Dec 1944.   Christmas Day. Work all day. Lowsy. At teatime thick rice and stew. From Canteen 5 small pineapples, 6 corncobs, 14 sweets, 12 bananas. No service. No celebrations. But thoughts very much with you.

And even New Year, an occasion recognised by the Japanese, was no better.

31 Dec 1944.   Camp cleaned up. Issue of a bit of orange peel jam at tea. Conditions seem to have deteriorated lately. It's more work and less time off. Still it'll soon be time to go home.

1 Jan 1945.   No general holiday this year. All work and no play. Cheers - two letters Mum 13/2/44 and 27/2/44.

Lionel's diary reveals that in the opening weeks of 1945 he had long hours of work in a sugar factory, doing night shifts. In this period he speaks of frequent air raids, unexpected arrivals and departures which left 320 British prisoners in the camp. Daily he uses the word *"fair"*, which in his usage of words meant "harsh and difficult". The bleak picture is lightened only by references to the receipt of a few letters from home. These served to take his mind off the deteriorating conditions.

His major problem was his health. He refers to having aching bones, back pains, a poisoned thumb, malaria and dysentery, and a brief time in the camp hospital.

25 Jan 1945. *In hospital in the evening with fever. Tummy off colour. Lowsy night. Not at work at night.*
26 Jan 1945. *Bit better. Out of hospital in evening.*

In spite of his habit of playing down his health problems it is clear that he was now at an all time low. But worse was to follow. One month after working all night in the sugar factory he returned to have his breakfast of two bananas when the siren sounded, and he could hear the bombs falling closer and closer.

7 Feb 1945. *Yanks bombed our camp. Don't know why. 13 killed and 65 wounded. Me head and back. Shaken, not bad. 7 Nips killed.*
8 Feb 1945. *8 more died during night.*

The writing, up to now written in ink, is in faint pencil, and some words are indistinct. Behind these brief words was a disaster for the P.O.W. camp. The fighter bombers had come right over Takao Camp. There had been a deafening explosion, and bombs had landed directly onto the camp. Lionel's head felt red hot and blood poured down his face. A colleague who had been sitting beside him to have breakfast collapsed beside him on the floor motionless. There was a deathly silence throughout the camp - some prisoners lay lifeless in the barracks, while others were groaning from their wounds.

His precious diary which he always kept concealed in his rucksack had been hit by shrapnel - the pages were torn in one corner and crumpled. That morning he had had a close brush with death. God had more work for him to do. Was more bombing to come? Would he survive the war?

His diary reveals continuing back pains through the injury received in the raid, further stomach trouble, almost daily bombings and diminishing food rations. On 15th February he reminds himself that he has been a prisoner now for three years - "*a very long time. Hoping for only a few weeks now.*" It was this optimism about the end of the war being imminent which kept this weakened and sickly prisoner going, amid the daily struggle for survival, the constant dropping of bombs, and the shouts and ravings of the guards.

Then there were signs that there was another move afoot. It was to be a return to Taihoku, his first camp in Formosa.

9 Mar 1945. *Move coming off. Camp being packed up.*
10 Mar 1945. *Think move to-morrow.*
11 Mar 1945. *Moved 5 p.m. ...We carry on to the 1st camp was at.*
12 Mar 1945. *Arrived 9.30 a.m. Met many old friends. Padre still here. Tummy very queer. Camp seems much better than we knew it Nov. 43.*

Haylor was back in Taihoku Camp on the north west of Formosa. It was to be his last move as a prisoner. His seven months at Takao had been the worst period of his imprisonment. Lifting heavy stones shoulder high on to trucks was beyond his physical strength after three years of malnutrition. After the more relaxed atmosphere of Taichu Camp relationships with the Japanese had been tense and precarious. The bombing of the camp had proved to be the last straw, leaving him with pieces of shrapnel embedded in his back. The prisoner was now suffering from many of the diseases associated with undernourishment. But somehow he felt the end was in sight.

Chapter 7.
Surviving the Last Lap.

(Taihoku Camp – 12/3/45 to 6/9/45)

For the entire period in which Haylor was back in Taihoku Camp, his vitality was low and his health in a critical state. His diary spoke of constant fever, of his legs and arms being weak, of swollen feet, stomach trouble, of a *"bad head"*, and of *"feeling very peculiar"*. He is constantly taking beri beri powder and vitamin tablets; and for much of this time he is on light manual work.

Almost daily American B24 and P38 bombers were flying over the camp bombing military installations and war factories in the capital city Taihoku nearby, though unfortunately the bombs were also killing many Formosan civilians and damaging many private homes. The sight of these planes assured the emaciated prisoners that their relief and liberation could not be far off.

The inmates were aware of the good news of V-E Day in Europe. On 30th April Lionel wrote, *"Think European affair finish"*. But closer to home significant things were also happening. News reached them that the Americans had attacked Okinawa. To the hundreds of prisoners languishing in the Formosan camps this development in the war represented important news. It meant that in the Allied advance from South East Asia towards Japan their island had been by-passed. The plot to massacre all prisoners in the event of an invasion of Formosa now receded, though such a massacre could still take place when Japan surrendered. The immediate danger of being killed had now subsided. News had somehow reached the Formosan camps that when the Japanese were retreating in the Philippines the prisoners had been massacred, atrocities had been committed and thousands of civilians had been killed.

As this time in Taihoku proceeded the prisoners found themselves walking a tightrope between life and death, between sanity and lunacy and between man and animal. An American prisoner at Shirakawa Camp had written these words -

> *How long, O Lord, can men endure the fate*
> *Of blasted hopes, defeat and vengeful hate?*
> *How long can spirit live and will survive?*
> *And keep the flickering flame of life alive*
> *In thralldom dark, depressed with ankering care,*
> *How long can hope contend with black despair?* [1]

One blessing which came out of this critical period was the degree of SHARING in Taihoku Camp to an extent hitherto unknown. They found themselves sharing the little extras that by good fortune came one prisoner's way, the sharing of moments of depression and desperation, the sharing of anxieties about the family back in Britain, and sharing of names and addresses of the wife or loved one in case death preceded liberation, the sharing of physical symptoms and discomfort. At this traumatic stage of imprisonment Lionel is both helping and being helped -

> *23 Apr 1945. J.G. looking after me. Very grateful. Hoping to regain strength very quickly.*
> *24 Apr 1945. Given two sweets at work. Tom gave me shirt and shorts.*

---

[1] - Part of "A Prisoner's Prayer" written by a senior American officer at Shirakawa, Formosa. Quoted by J. Edwards, *Banzai you Bastards* - pp. 184, 185.

22 Jun 1945.   Pat White a bit ill. Trying and succeeding in cheering him up.

Every few days the diary records another death. It was tragic to think that these men had survived the ordeals of Changi Camp and the years in Formosa, to die within a few months of liberation. The entire camp was going slowly downhill in health and vitality. In his characteristic way of playing down the appalling conditions at this time, Lionel simply says –

7 Aug 1945.   Bit of increase in sickness in camp.
10 Aug 1945. Health of camp not too good. Feeling very peculiar.

It is clear that the Taihoku inmates could not continue this life and death struggle much longer. Over three years of undernourishment and unhygienic living conditions were now rapidly taking their toll. And it was just at this crucial time that the war came to an abrupt and decisive end with America dropping atomic bombs on Hiroshima and Nagasaki on 6th and 9th August respectively. On 10th August Japan surrendered to the Allies, though the formal surrender did not take place until 2nd September.

What Laurens van der Post says in his *The Night of the New Moon* about the importance of these events to the prisoner of war camps in Java and South East Asia applies also to those in Formosa –

> The war would have dragged on, and apart from many many more Japanese dead, hundreds and thousands of Americans and their Allies would have died as well, and hundreds of thousands of prisoners would have been killed. Even if we had not been deliberately massacred, we were near our physical end through lack of food. The war had only to drag on some months longer for most of us to have perished. [2]

In Taihoku Camp, although the specific news of the dropping of the atomic bombs had not reached the prisoners, they soon became aware that something had happened. Lionel records –

17 Aug 1945.   Party sent to straighten cemetery out. Conference between Commandant and our officer. Issue of sweets and bottle juice per man. Rice ration doubled. Issue of Red Cross tinned biscuits and cheese. Not told war is over but we suspect.
18 Aug 1945.   Given news at night that war over on 14/15th. What a feeling of relief to be free. Yank authorities expected 20/21 ...What a change in Nips towards us. Nearly licking our boots.

Various groups of prisoners were being brought from all over the island to Taihoku, which at the time of liberation had some 1,200 inmates. Low as Lionel and his colleagues were in health and physical condition, they had a shock when they saw the 140 men who had arrived from Hill Camp.

21 Aug 1945.   Arrival 5 p.m. of rest of our lads. Mere skeletons - indescribable. It

---

[2] - p.144 *The Night Of The New Moon* by Laurens van der Post.

even appals us and we are used to most things. The sight of these lads makes blood boil.

Most of the inmates of Taihoku Camp were now ill with disease and malnutrition, and only the vague knowledge that the war was finishing kept these thin and emaciated men going. Daily they watched the movements of the Japanese for any indication that they were abandoning control of the camp. Lionel noted in his diary his surprise and satisfaction on seeing Japanese guards doing various camp jobs, such as feeding the livestock and clearing away the rubbish. The inmates made a point of not demonstrating their glee about the Allied victory, and they avoided going near the guards' huts. They did, however, feel bold enough to sing the National Anthem at the Sunday service on 26th August.

They had been told that the Americans would be arriving by air to release them, and bringing much needed supplies. With no heavy labour to do they spent the time washing and drying their tattered clothes, and discussing their prospects of being home for Christmas. They watched the sky for the liberators, and were not kept waiting long. On the afternoon of 28th August three B29s circled over the camp. On their underwings were the words "P.W. Supplies". Lionel describes that day as *"the greatest day yet"*. After recording in his diary the arrival of the three planes in the sky, he write, *"The lads went potty"*. Leaflets announcing the capitulation of Japan fluttered down on the trees and on to the fields. The B29s swooped low and dropped 150-litre drums loaded with food - inside were supplies of chocolate, biscuits, tinned fruit and fruit juice.

But there was a sadder side to this eventful day. One plane flew so low that the parachutes carrying drums did not open, and the drums hit the camp hospital, killing three men and injuring 21. This was a blot on an otherwise happy day.

Planes with food and clothes continued to come almost daily. Chalked on one drum of supplies were the words, "Can't take you this time. Perhaps next?" The food was distributed promptly among the prisoners, and soon the daily meals were infinitely more nutritious; and rice of which they had become tired was phased out of the menu. But the increased vitamin meals could not affect a quick-fix on the thin and feeble bodies of the prisoners. Recovery could only come in gradual stages as their bodies got used to changed food. Lionel had a fresh bout of fever, and felt frustrated that he could not tackle the improved meals.

On Sunday 2nd September, described in the diary as *"another GREAT occasion"*, two U.S. Naval officers and two Chinese officers, all armed to the teeth, arrived in Taihoku with the task of tending to the welfare of the P.O.W.s. That same day at the Communion Service the padre led the small congregation in prayers of thanksgiving to God for the ending of the war. Later the Japanese Commandant gave a speech to the assembled prisoners, wishing them a happy return to their homes. Then Major Crossley disarmed the Japanese and gave the rifles to a newly formed guard from among the prisoners. On Tuesday, 4th September, Lionel wrote his first letter home, free from restrictions and censorship. He certainly had much to write home about. Everything was moving fast and furiously, and every new development brought excitement and keen anticipation of leaving the camp soon.

On 6th September they finally departed. Lionel described it as *"the greatest day yet"*. Some marines had arrived the day before from an aircraft carrier. They now asked the men to line up outside their huts and leave everything behind. But habits die hard. After three years of acute shortages they instinctively dragged out with them some of the primitive cutlery and unused food from their huts. The marine gently repeated his instructions. "Leave everything behind." This time they obliged, looking back wistfully at the "treasures" they had abandoned.

They boarded the train at Taihoku station. From there they could see that the capital city had taken a battering from the American bombers in recent months. At the platform the local civilians cheered and waved as they boarded for their short journey. There were even a few Japanese soldiers standing passively in the crowd. Their officers had mysteriously disappeared. At every halt and crossing the released prisoners were cheered by the local populace. As they drew into Keelung station they could see around it all the destruction to buildings and properties which the raids had brought in the previous year.

For a few moments they were standing on the same quayside at Keelung where they had arrived after that gruesome voyage from Changi in November, 1942. Much had happened since that unforgettable day - moves from one camp to another, health crises, the deaths of comrades - a flood of memories both good and bad. The dock-side was cordoned off with barbed wire, and armed American sentries were standing in line. The sailors welcomed them as they arrived. They were receiving VIP treatment. Lionel pinched himself - was he dreaming? Would he wake up in his squalid hut in Taihoku? No, it was real life.

The men boarded an American destroyer which took them to an aircraft carrier - the *USN Santee* - which was waiting out at sea. They were helped aboard, soon to be divested of their ragged clothes. A hot bath and a shave with a new shaving set, and the issue of new clothes - a sailor's cap, shirt and trousers. They felt like princes. Lionel gave an enthusiastic account in his diary -

> *6 Sept 1945.   Scrumptious meal ... It's great. Everyone trotting around us like children, willing to do this, that and the other for us. It's lovely being looked after by Navy. Well, must write to you, so here's starting.*

What he wrote from the comfort and luxury of that American ship can be imagined.

That evening the aircraft carrier sailed away from Keelung. The coast of Formosa slowly receded from sight. A flood of memories flashed through Haylor's mind - Taihoku ... Taichu ... Takao... It had been a terrible war. Millions had died, and millions of others had suffered its ravages. Would the nations learn to live together peaceably?

> *Why can't the wheat be divided?*
> *And the soldiers sent home?*
> *And the barriers torn down?*
> *And the enemies forgiven?*
> *And there be no retribution?* [3]

Before going to sleep in his camp bed with clean sheets and blankets on the hangar deck Lionel thought about the coming months. How soon would his health improve? What

---

[3] Stephen Spender, *The War God*.

adjustments would he have to make returning to the modern world? Would he be fit to return to his job at the Romford Post Office? After all that he had been through would Joan find that he had changed?

These and other important questions flooded his mind. But then he returned to the things which eclipsed these anxieties. He was going to a life of freedom after three years of captivity. He was returning to family, to friends, to love and understanding ... and so the period of adjustment which lay ahead of him would be made easier. Above all, his prayers through those dark and difficult days had been abundantly answered.

> *I love the Lord, because He hath heard my voice and my supplications.*
> *The sorrows of death compassed me, and the pains of Hell gat hold upon me. I found trouble and sorrow. Then called I upon the name of the Lord.*
> *Return unto thy rest, O my soul, for the Lord hath dealt bountifully with thee. For Thou hast delivered my soul from death,*
> > *mine eyes from tears*
> > *and my feet from falling.*
> *I will walk before the Lord in the land of the living.*
> > > (Psalm 116, vv 1-9)

Epilogue

The final story of rehabilitation for some returning ex-POWs was not a happy one. For them the traumas of the war years could not be shaken off that easily. Adjusting once again to "civvy street" and to family and friends proved to be too much for them.

But for Lionel Haylor all went relatively smoothly, though recovery was slow. In Joan Walker he was to have a helpmeet who showed love, understanding and patience. While waiting for his return she had undergone courses in medicine and psychology, and was well equipped to nurse a returned soldier back to normality.

Let us go back to Lionel's arrival back in Britain. On the 3rd December, 1945, the "Andes", a 26,000 ton passenger liner, docked at Southampton. On board were several hundred former prisoners of war. Their return to their homes was done efficiently and expeditiously. A train took Lionel to the Baker Street station in central London. Then a lorry ride to Liverpool Street station, and a final train journey to Romford. At last he was back in his old stamping ground. The welcome he received from his family and from Joan after the five long anxious years of separation can be imagined - the swopping of yarns in the weeks that followed, chatting and reminiscing into the night, the laughter and yes, also the tears.

Looking back Lionel sees the advantage in taking three months to get back to Britain from Formosa (now Taiwan) via Australia. To-day a returning prisoner is flown home within 24 hours of release, but the speedy return carries with it the difficulty of adjusting to a new way of life so quickly. In his circuitous journey home Lionel received careful medical treatment and issues of clothing, and in the process had time to ponder over the changes which lay ahead. For years his every move had been regimented, his life tightly supervised and all decisions had been made for him. He had now to prepare himself for the fast moving world from which he had been separated when struggling for survival in the make-shift huts of Formosa.

Back in Essex recovery came slowly and steadily. The month of January found him in the Colchester Military Hospital. Bouts of shivering meant that the malaria of Taihoku days was continuing to trouble him. On the other hand his weight since his release had nearly doubled. The skin and bones prisoner of 7½ stone now weighed 13½ stone. Also, the shrapnel in his back from the American air raid had to be removed.

On 9th February, 1946, Lionel and Joan were married in the South Street Congregational Church, Romford. The building itself was a reminder of the recent war and its air raids. There was only one door through which both the bridal procession and the congregation could enter, and as the bride and bridegroom made their vows they were confronted by a pile of scaffolding and timber at the front. But all this made little difference to the happiness of the wedding day. The military authorities had instructed Lionel to undergo some medical examinations just at the time of the marriage with a view to giving him his discharge, but to keep his date with Joan Lionel had persuaded his superiors to postpone their plans. They had waited for this happy day for too long.

In October, 1946, Lionel was back at his work in the Post Office. He was later to move to H.M. Customs & Excise. The newly weds worked together in the South Street Sunday School. Lionel was later made a deacon in the church, and then Treasurer of the church, which in its present building is now known as the Western Road United Reformed Church. Lionel Haylor strongly believes that while some are called to preach and teach, there is much practical work for others with different skills. This has been his contribution.

It is now half a century since the events recounted in this book took place. Daphne (born in May, 1947), Maureen (born February, 1949) and John (born June, 1950) have grown up, and there are six grandchildren. It is my hope and prayer that this story of courage, faith and endurance will inspire them and all who read this book to keep faith with God even when "the chips are down", as Lionel Haylor did.

The Wedding of Lionel and Joan Haylor
9th February, 1946
at the Congregational Church, Romford.

Appendices

Appendix 1. Numerical Strength of Changi P.O.W. Camp 17/2/42 – 31/10/43

Date	Strength	Date	Strength
17/2/42	41,500	31/12/42	26,374
18/2/42	52,200	28/2/43	28,207
31/3/42	45,562	31/3/43	22,235
30/4/42	31,997	30/4/43	10,564
31/5/42	16,818	31/5/43	5,500
30/6/42	15,445	30/6/43	5,359
31/7/42	17,028	31/7/43	5,381
31/8/42	18,790	31/8/43	5,307
31/10/42	15,744	30/9/43	5,332
30/11/42	10,924	31/10/43	6,819

Source: *"The Story of Changi"* by D. Nelson

Appendix 2. Selerang Special Order No. 3 dated 4th Sept. 1942

1. On 30th Aug. 1942 I together with my Area Commanders was summoned to the Conference House, Changi Gaol, where I was informed by the representative of Maj. Gen. Shimpei Fukuye (G.O.C./ P.O.W. Camps Malaya) that all P.O.W.s in Changi Camp were to be given forms of promise not to escape, and that all were to be given an opportunity to sign this form.
2. By the Laws and Usages of War a Prisoner of War cannot be required by the Power holding him to give his parole, and in our Army those who became P.O.W.s are not to be permitted to give their parole. I pointed out this position to the Japanese Authorities.
3. I informed the representative of Maj. Gen. Shimpei Fukuye that I was not prepared to sign the form, and that I did not consider that any Officer or man in Changi Camp would be prepared to sign the form. In accordance with the orders of the Japanese Authorities all P.O.W.s were given an opportunity to sign. The result of that opportunity is well known.
4. On 31st Aug. I was informed by the Japanese Authorities that those personnel who refused to sign the certificate would be subjected to "measures of severity", and that a refusal to sign would be regarded as a direct refusal to obey a regulation which the I.J.A. considered it necessary to enforce.
5. Later, on the night of 31st Aug./1st Sept. I was warned that on 1st Sept. all P.O.W.s persisting in refusing to sign were to move by 1800 hrs. to Selarang barrack square. I confirmed both on my own behalf and in the name of the P.O.W.s our refusal to sign.
6. The move to Selarang Barrack Square was accomplished on the same afternoon.
7. I and the Area Commander have been in constant conference with the I.J.A. and have endeavoured by negotiation to have the form either abolished or at least modified. All that I have been able to obtain is that which was originally a demand, accompanied by threats of "measures of severity", has now been issued as an official order of the Imperial Japanese Government.
8. During the period of occupation of Selerang Barrack Square the conditions in which we have been placed have been under my constant consideration. These may be briefly described as such that existence therein will result in a very few days in the outbreak of epidemic and the most serious consequences to those under my command, and the inevitable death of many. Taking into account the low state of health in which many of us now are, and the need to preserve our force intact as long as possible, and in the full conviction that my action, were the circumstances in which we are now living known to them, would meet with the approval of His Majesty's Government, I have felt it my duty to ORDER all personnel to sign the certificate under duress imposed by the I.J.A.
9. I am fully convinced that His Majesty's Government only expects P.O.W.s not to give their parole when such parole is to be given voluntarily. This factor can in no circumstances be applicable to our present position. The responsibility for this decision rests with me and with me alone, and I fully accept it in ordering you to sign.
10. I wish to record in this order my deep appreciation of the excellent spirit and good discipline which all ranks have shown during this trying period. I look to all ranks to

continue in good heart, discipline and morale. Thank you all for your loyalty and co-operation.

Signed. E.B.HOLMES Colonel

Comd. British and Australian troops Changi.

SELERANG

4th Sept. 1942.

COPY OF LETTER No. SELERANG 11/A 4.9.42

Ref. SELERANG Special Order No.3 dated 4th Sept. 1942.

My attention has been drawn to some concern which is being felt that there may be adverse financial consequences on individuals as a result of the signing of the non-escape certificate.

It is obviously impossible for me to give a ruling in this matter which must rest in other hands than mine. I wish, however, all ranks to be informed that this point had my full consideration at the time of the decision, and I am convinced that no such adverse consequences on pay, pension or allowance will result to any individual. It will naturally be my first endeavour also to ensure on release that the position is made clear to His Majesty's Government.

Signed. E.B.HOLMES Colonel

Comd. British and Australian troops Changi.

CHANGI

4.9.1942.

Note: I.J.A. = Imperial Japanese Army

Appendix 3. (Continued). The Japanese Order to kill all Formosan P.O.W.s.

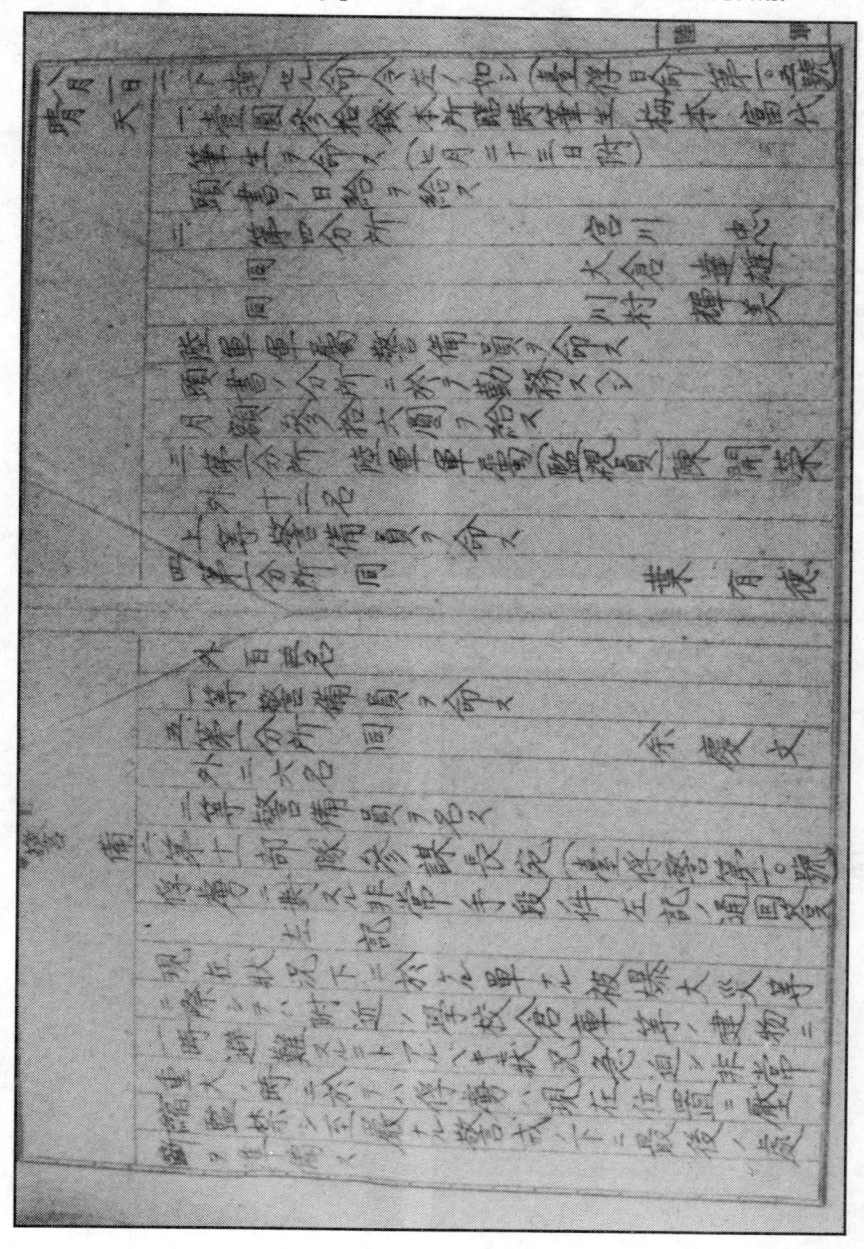

Appendix 3 (Continued) The Japanese Order to kill all Formosan P.O.W.s.

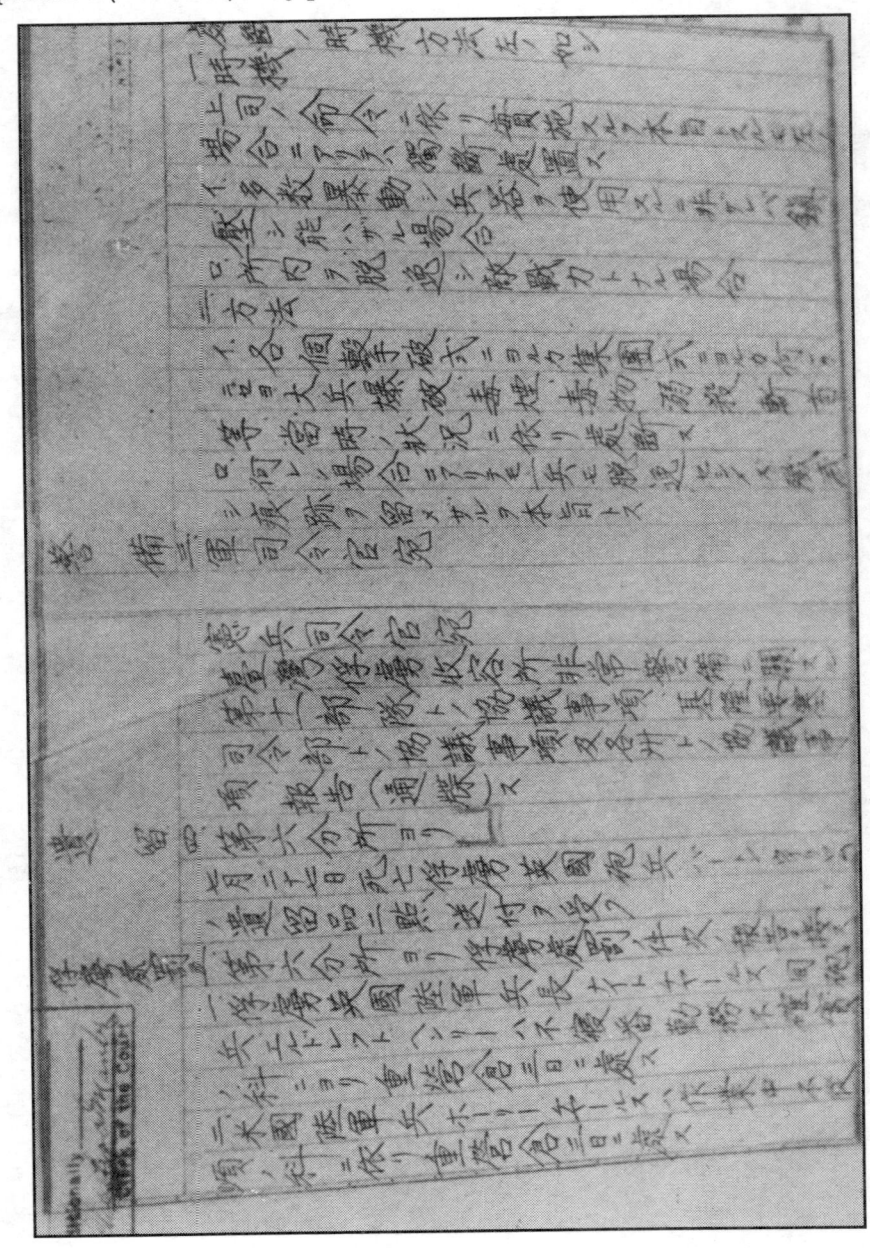

Appendix 3. Continued. Translation of the above.

The Japanese Order to kill all P.O.W.s in Formosa

In response to your enquiries concerning emergency procedures in respect of Prisoners of War, please note the following:

Under the present circumstances, if there is heavy bombing all prisoners should be evacuated to a nearby school or store house. However, if the situation becomes critically dangerous, the prisoners should be confined to where they already are. They should be strictly guarded, and you must be ready to perform the "final deed".

The timing and the method of committing the "final deed" -

Timing. Although this decision should normanlly be made on the authority of a high ranking officer, the situation may develop to a point where a guard will have to make his own judgment, such as -

(a) When a large number of prisoners riot, and it is deemed impossible to control and suppress such a riot, the use of arms would be legitimate,

(b) If prisoners attempted to escape or are found to be co-operating with enemy forces.

Method. Having decided to kill, the method used will depend on the circumstances -

(a) This could be by the use of a bomb, poisonous gas, poison in the food, of drwoning or of beheading. This could be done individually or en masse.

(b) Whatever is done, it is important that no one escapes, that all are totally killed and no trace is left behind afterwards.

Appendix 4. Obituary to John Burns Leech
A True Soldier

As he was about to be promoted to Bugle Major in 1934, John Burns Leech left the Army he had joined as a 16 year-old Wandsworth lad twelve years previously. Upon enlistment as a boy recruit he had been posted to India where he spent his total twelve years service. Two wonderful things happened during that service: he was led to Christ by a fellow-soldier at the age of 20, and two years later received a call from God to serve Him in India as soon as his "time" expired. With very little normal education background before enlistment, he had worked hard throughout his army years to build upon a natural inquisitiveness and acquisitiveness, and thus prepare himself for the Lord's service. After two years in the Missionary Training College, the R.B.M.U. sent him out to North India in 1936. There he worked until the wartime emergency called him back to army service again.

Lieutenant J. B. Leech was among those captured at Singapore and spent four years in Japanese captivity. This captivity was also marked by two outstanding things: firstly, by his courageous witness and spiritual ministry to his fellow prisoners, and secondly, by the privation and malnutrition that produced the severe arthritic condition which eventually led to his death. I well remember the day at the end of 1945 when, on a visit to the Chaplain's House in Lucknow, I discovered John just returned from the Japanese prison camp with one of his arms in plaster and in a sling at right-angles to his shoulder. Throughout the years that followed the arthritis spread over his body, hardly leaving a joint unaffected, invading for periods both sight and hearing, limiting his movement in a ruthless increase from year to year and inflicting incessant pain.

He returned to the Bihar Field in 1948 and gave 12 years' more service, taking a great part in the Mission's anti-leprosy work and undertaking the translation and production of the Scripture Union Notes in Hindi for six years. In both of these spheres he set standards of devotion and efficiency which were typical of his deep love for the Lord Jesus Christ, and we thank God for this ministry which was exercised in constant physical suffering of an intensity that would have completely frustrated a lesser spirit. He was preparing to return to the Field after furlough in Canada in March, 1961, when he was suddenly stricken down by some vicious complication of his arthritis, and his rallying from that crisis was a miracle to all who saw him. In March this year (1962) I saw him in the hospital in London, Ontario, still almost completely immobile a year after that crisis, but his mood and spirit were certainly not immobile. Two things stand out from my visit that day: firstly, his rebuking of me that the R.M.B.U. had not done more for Radio Evangelism in India, work of which he was an untiring advocate, and secondly, his conviction that God would send him back to India. As I accepted the rebuke it was reasonable to accept his conviction also, and so it was a surprise to be cabled of his passing on May 7th. He was a true soldier of Jesus Christ, intent on pleasing Him Who had called him.

This testimony would not be complete without mention of Bessie Steen of Canada, whom John married in early 1939. The story of her faith and courage throughout the silent years of John's imprisonment, of her support to him in all his pain and disability, and the unfailing supply of that part of his ministry of which he was physically incapable, is an epic of our Indian Field. In giving thanks for John's ministry we commit to prayerful fellowship Bessie and their children, Patricia, Ian, David and Andrew.

E. W. OLIVER
(R.B.M.U. magazine)

Appendix 5. Lionel Haylor's weight – 16/9/42 – 31/1/46

Date	Weight	Notes
16/9/42	9st. 9lbs	Changi Camp. Red Cross parcels arrived soon afterwards – 13/10/42
17/1/43	8st. 9lbs	Taihoku Camp
28/3/43	9st. 1lb	Taihoku Camp. Red Cross parcels arrived 11/4/43
25/7/43	8st. 11lbs	Taihoku Camp. Desperate need for greens
19/11/43	9st. –	Taichu Camp
26/12/43	9st. 5lbs	Taichu Camp. Good food on Christmas Day
16/1/44	8st. 11lbs	Taichu Camp. Receiving powder for beri beri
27/3/44	9st. 1lb	Taichu Camp. General shortage of food in Formosa
29/4/44	8st. 11lbs	Taichu Camp
28/5/44	9st. –	Taichu Camp
23/7/44	8st. 11lbs	Takao Camp
20/8/44	8st. 12 lbs	Takao Camp
23/12/44	7st. 9lbs	Takao Camp. Christmas – low rations
2/3/45	8st. –	Takao Camp
18/3/45	7st. 8lbs	Taihoku Camp. Food critically short
22/4/45	7st. 12 lbs	Taihoku Camp
20/5/45	7st. 10lbs	Taihoku Camp
24/6/45	7st. 10lbs	Taihoku Camp
19/8/45	7st. 6lbs	Taihoku Camp. Lowest weight just before release
11/9/45	8st. 10lbs	Taihoku Camp. After release. Supplies of food being dropped by air
31/1/46	13st. 7lbs	Britain. Four months of good food.

Source: L. Haylor's Diary